Nice Work, Boys!

Gaining Confidence and Learning to Lead, One Job at a Time

Hanalei Souza

Nice Work, Boys!: Gaining Confidence and Learning to Lead, One Job at a Time.

Copyright © 2021 Hanalei Souza

Independently Published

Paperback ISBN 978-1-7367897-0-4
ebook ISBN: 978-1-7367897-1-1
Library of Congress Control Number: 2021909360

Names, places, and in some cases, minor identifying details have been changed to keep anonymity.

Author contact:
www.ladylinecook.com

Cover design by Jake Eames
www.jakeeames.com

First edition

To my husband and best friend, Gavin

To my parents

CONTENTS

INTRODUCTION

My first promotion at any job ever was in a workplace of about thirty men and one woman (me). It was a job at a ski resort in Mountain Operations, or "Mountain Ops," which meant physical labor, long hours, big machines, power tools, and lots of time on snow in all conditions. Overall, I learned so much from my time there, and I'm grateful for that experience and time in my life. I was twenty-one years old, had no leadership experience, was working seventy to eighty hours a week, and had to face a bully and two serious injuries, all within a few short months. I had to learn life skills "on the fly," as they say in restaurants. At the end of that ski season, I knew I wanted to capture that experience in writing and recount everything I had learned in such a short time. I started writing that story but didn't know what to do with it.

After that experience, I found my place in restaurant kitchens and encountered the same gender demographic. It's not like I was looking for male-dominated fields for the sake of it. Those were the types of jobs I wanted to work, and I didn't want to let that get in the way. Representation is great, but sometimes we have to get out there and be the only one of our kind, even if we're the first one we've seen in that field.

Equipped with the experience from that first leadership job, I started in the kitchen with a thick skin and an open mind. The kitchen taught me even more lessons on leadership, humility, and life. I fell in love with the rush, the camaraderie, and the ways it continued to challenge me as a cook and as a person. Writing was often my after-work outlet. Some of these pages were written at 2 a.m. after a brutal Saturday night service, still covered in grease, sweat, and chicken juice, eating ice cream for dinner and trying to process what just happened. I loved capturing the madness of a dinner rush with words on a page. I wanted to bring readers into the kitchen, right there next to me, flipping steaks and slinging mussels diablo on a holiday weekend. I wrote about my frustrations, my wins, and my losses. I didn't know who or what it was for; I just wanted to write it.

When I began leading in the kitchen, I was able to draw parallels between my ski resort job and my new workplace. I was able to build upon what I learned and experienced there as a supervisor. I faced many of the same struggles but was able to see it with a different perspective. That's when I put the pieces together and started this book. I know there is still so much more for me to learn, and there are lessons I talk about here that I know I still need to practice in action.

We all have a lens we view our world through. It's how we cope with what life throws our way. For me, it is my Christian faith. I have had a personal relationship with Christ since eighth grade, and my faith has played an integral part in my identity and how I dealt with the events in this book. Whether you share my beliefs or not, this book is just my story.

In both fields I worked in, I heard one phrase often thrown my way. On the mountain, I would be working right under the chairlift with the guys. "Nice work, boys!" someone would call from the chairlift. "Nice work, boys!" they'd say while skiing past our crew working on getting the halfpipe ready to open for the public.

I was usually stoked to hear this comment. I didn't bother correcting them. I took it as a compliment. Plus, we all had helmets, baggy clothes, and ski goggles on. In fact, most times a coworker would immediately correct them, and shout, "and girl!" It made me feel like they were proud of me and my work, and that I was one of them when they did this. I felt recognized.

In the kitchen, I'd hear it first during a slammin' Saturday lunch service.

"Nice work, boys!" said one of the waiters as he picked up the food for his table.

Without skipping a beat, the head chef, who was on the line next to the rest of us, said, "You're going to have to start saying 'nice work, boys and girls' now!"

While all events are true as remembered, we all know memory is subjective and reflects the interpretation of the author. Some dialogue consistent with the nature and character of the person depicted has been recreated, and names, places, and in some cases, minor identifying details have been changed to keep anonymity.

CHAPTER 1

A Woman's Place

Out of all the places I could be on a holiday weekend night, why here? I thought, as I squeeze-bottled lines of red pepper sauce over a seafood tagliarini dish. (Oh, squeeze bottles, what would we cooks ever do without them?) I couldn't think about how weeded I was, or the heat, or the fresh burn bubbles going all the way up my arm. In restaurant speak, "weeded" or "being in the weeds" means slammed, way behind, struggling to stay on top of the rush. Imagine you're juggling, but people keep throwing you balls, and you have to keep juggling all of them. Then the balls catch fire, but you can't stop. And people keep telling you, "I need that ball now! How long before you're done?"

I glanced over to the corner of the kitchen, where a server was rolling silverware and chatting up a storm. She seemed so tranquil, a cool cucumber compared to the madness of the line. In the less than half a second I spent in silverware Zen-land with the server, I thought, *What I'd do right now to be there, with not a care in the world except rolling silverware.* I shifted my focus back. I couldn't focus on how weeded I was; I just had to keep cooking. *Next pickup: three sea bass, two seafood pasta, a cowboy steak special, and three airline chicken.* Focusing on that next pickup was the small thread I hung on to, to keep from drowning in a sea of paper tickets.

Women are expected to cook at home for their family, not in a tough, physically arduous, mentally exhausting, balls-to-the-wall-paced, no-screw-ups-allowed, male-dominated restaurant kitchen.

Why do the people who say "A woman's place is the kitchen" usually think this is true unless it's a professional kitchen, where, instead of cooking for a few friends and family members, she's cooking for hundreds, maybe even a thousand paying customers with high standards?

Where, instead of having plenty of time to cook one big casserole for everyone, she's cooking to order big-ticket entrees, and has only fifteen minutes to cook each dish?

Where she might be the only woman and may even be in charge of leading a team through a dinner rush?

If a woman can cook, they call her "wifey material." If she cooks at a restaurant, they say, "You're too pretty to work back there. You should be taking my order."

"So, you're like a prep helper or a cake decorator, right?"

"You should work cold stations and dessert. You wouldn't want to get burns from working the grill."

"Can you make sure it's a man who cooks my steak?"

"That's nice, sweetie, but can I talk to the chef?"

"Women can't put in the same hours men can."

These are all real quotes, by the way, that I collected from other female cooks and chefs.

"I bet you make great tips there as a waitress," they say, after I've told them where I work as a *cook* and have just finished a busy holiday weekend. It stings a little harder when you are at a place that does not tip out the kitchen, which is quite common.

That night I found myself *in the weeds*, plating up seafood pastas and trying to keep my focus away from the server in silverware land, was one of those busy holidays. I was covering for the main sauté cook over Labor Day weekend while he was out for a few weeks for an unavoidable family situation. Every station in the kitchen has its own hardships, but sauté was definitely the most intricate, and only a few cooks could work it. Just when I thought I was holding it down pretty well, the orders coming in at a decent pace, the ticket printer started rattling off like a machine gun and didn't stop for three hours.

Early on in that rush, I hastily and carelessly dropped a skin-on airline chicken breast into smoking-hot oil in a pan and it splashed everywhere. I knew oil splattered all over my arm, but I didn't feel any burns; that's the kind of adrenaline you're on during a four-hundred-cover night (covers meaning how many people came through the restaurant, in this case between 5 and 10 p.m. Four hundred butts in the chairs. Four hundred people ordering appetizers, main courses, and desserts). I was cranking out sea bass entrée after sea bass entrée—having five to seven of those working at any given time throughout the night. I was plating up prime rib sides and seafood pasta dishes to the tune of whirring hood vents, crashing dishes, and the chef calling out our next pickup.

I had all twelve stove burners on and both ovens full. I didn't have time for pain. And the heat? I wasn't even thinking about the heat, even though it was a late-summer evening, cooped up in a windowless, stainless-steel dungeon, reaching into a 450-degree oven every five minutes. At 10 p.m., when the rush calmed down, I showed a server my burns. His jaw hit the floor.

"A grease splash? You look like you pinned your whole arm to the grill!"

I still have the scars as I write this.

So yes, please keep telling me that cooking is a "woman's job," or that a man who can cook is displaying "feminine" qualities. Please keep telling me that my place is the kitchen, because it is. But if you're going to use it as an insult or some sort of way to assert dominance as a man, I *dare* you to find the busiest restaurant in your city on a day when the line is out the door, peek into the kitchen, and watch. You might not even see a woman, and if you do, you better believe she's tough as nails.

***

My first restaurant job was at a place I'll call the "seafood spot" in the quaint downtown area of the town I had just moved to. Although it was a mountain town far away from any ocean, the owners had the plug on some high-quality, overnight-shipped seafood, and the restaurant specialized in lobster rolls and fresh-butchered fish, featuring a tank of live lobsters, red picnic benches, and clam "chowdah" in a bread bowl.

Cooking at a restaurant was almost a bucket list item to check off or something I felt I had to get out of my system for a summer. I had no formal training, but I loved to cook at home, and that summer, I decided I would give it a go. Although I had been into cooking my whole life, I had never considered it as a career. As kids, we're encouraged to dream about what we want to be based on what we actually like. However, when we are in high school and have to actually think about what we are going to be, we are told to think of what would be sensible rather than what we "like to do." I remember saying that I "liked cooking and wanted to keep it that way," because "if I had to do it for work, I may end up hating it." I didn't know what I wanted, and I knew that, but it seems we are all pressured to decide at seventeen when we pick our college and major.

College is not the only option after high school, but in the academically focused area I grew up in, it was made to seem that way. I figured business was always a good move, because no matter what I did, there would always be a business component. After completing my senior year of high school at a community college, essentially skipping a year, I was able to transfer to my dream school up in the mountains to study business with a focus on the ski industry. I was one of three women in my major in my graduating class, so I knew what was ahead of me in the ski industry. I then finished college at twenty, moved to a ski town half an hour away from the college, worked a winter at a ski resort where I planned to return the following winter, and needed a summer job to tide me over until then.

The month I started at the seafood spot, May 2018, was a whirlwind of a month. Having just turned twenty-one, I attended my college graduation, finished up my first season in the ski industry, started at the seafood spot, and got married. I wasn't looking to get married at twenty-one. The concept of starting a family wasn't even a goal I would have listed growing up. I had my first date at nineteen, and I honestly thought I'd be the last one I knew to get married. I figured I would just do my thing, and if someone wanted to join in, I'd give him a chance.

We met during my junior year of college at a young-adult get-together hosted by an older Christian couple. I sat next to him and was drawn to his friendly and inviting demeanor, and how easily we kept talking—he about his summer adventures in Alaska, I about my summer work at a snowboarding camp. When we got each other's numbers and started hanging out, we found out we had already seen each other out on the ski hill the previous winter and had talked without exchanging names or numbers. It was almost as if God had given us a second chance at meeting after screwing up the first.

While other little girls played "family" and pretended their dolls were their kids, I played restaurant, and I was always the maitre d'. I was the eight-year old girl who did kung fu and kicked Barbies to the curb. My cousin made the fatal mistake of giving me a Barbie doll for Christmas when I was five. I threw a fit and told her how much I hated it. I think that was the day my parents gave me a lecture on how to accept a gift graciously, whether it's what I want or not.

At my elementary-school-age birthday parties, my parents would set up a "restaurant" with a menu of basic kids' food like frozen fish sticks or pasta. To a ten-year-old, it was basically a three-Michelin-starred affair.

Although I had an interest in food and restaurants as a child, eating at an actual one was, and still is, a once-a-year-treat. I was taught from a young age to always tip the server based on the original bill, not the bill after coupons and gift cards, which we always had. I was taught by my ninety-year-old Dutch grandma, who we called "Oms" to order steak rare or bleu (rarer than rare), when we went to one of those "steak on a stone" places where they give you a hot plate to cook your own steak, and I watched her give it a quick sear on each side like ahi tuna and dig in. Many people learn a special recipe from their grandma. Mine taught me how to eat a steak.

This lack of going to restaurants was mainly because both of my parents cooked. My mom did most of the cooking and taught me the basics, but my dad would often cook as well, introducing me to the finer side of food. I was born and raised in the United States, but I wouldn't say I grew up American. We ate every dinner at an actual dining table, as Europeans do, and we watched mainly British children's TV shows, like *Wallace and Gromit* or *Jellykins*. We were also a frugal household. We had a drawer full of used aluminum foil, twist ties from bread, and plastic bags in our house, and we would be scolded if we dared to use one of those items only once before throwing it away. My parents always drove cars to death, buying an already-used minivan when I was born, then legally teaching me to drive it sixteen years later. We never, ever, ever threw away food. We boiled any bones into stock.

We saved the parchment from butters and used them to grease pans, which was also something passed down from Oms, my bleu-steak-ordering grandma. She had learned frugality from her time in World War Two prisoner of war camps, but that time had also given her a sense of gratitude and appreciation in her postwar life. As a prisoner, she didn't even have the luxury of knowing that she would see the next day.

"I eat ice cream for dessert every day," she would say, scooping a nice dollop of vanilla ice cream into a bowl. "I didn't make it through prisoner of war camp to deny myself the simple pleasures of life."

For her, life is too short to cook your steak well done.

Although my entire family besides my parents and brother lived in the UK, we managed to see them at least every few years, even as adults. When my husband, Gavin, and I were dating and had saved up enough to go to the UK with my parents to visit the rest of my family, we were sitting at the dining table, eating "supper," as they say there, and Gavin was being a bit of a "loud American."

Oms held up her fork and told him, "Has anyone ever told you to fork off?"

We all laughed. That's when we knew he would fit right in with the family.

My other Grandma, Nai-Nai, from my mom's side was a soft-spoken, four-foot-ten, Burmese princess. My mom and her five siblings were born there in Burma, now Myanmar, and moved to the U.K. after political unrest and a military dictatorship drove them out. We didn't see Nai-Nai as much as we did Oms, but rumor has it she was an amazing cook. My mom talked about how she would cook with every single part of the animal and could debone an entire chicken while keeping it all intact. I've never been back to Burma, but I'd like to. I was even given a Burmese royalty name, *Lady Golden Palm*. Had political unrest never happened, I would probably be sitting on some Burmese throne made of gold, but there I was, applying for line cook jobs instead. I guess you can call me "lady garlic palm" for now.

My grandfathers both passed away when I was young, but I remember making bread with Oms's husband, who we called Tadcu. There's a story circulating from when my other grandpa, Nai-Nai's husband, was able to make a whole gourmet meal from only an onion and a bottle of gin. I was used to seeing both men and women cooking in the home, both from my parents and my grandparents

Whenever we would go back to England to visit my family, which was about once a year as a child, and less often as a teenager and adult after airline prices soared, we stayed at Oms's house in Crawley, a small town about an hour's train ride from London. It is the same house my father and his two siblings were born and raised in. That town feels like home, even though I never lived there. On street corners, there are those classic red phone booths and red mailboxes you see in movies. There is a park my brother and I would always walk to and play on the flying fox—a seat attached to a rope that slid down a cable about a hundred feet long. That kind of unregulated park feature would never exist in the United States—too many lawsuits.

It was at my grandma's Crawley house where I cooked my first Christmas dinner. I was fourteen. I had been cooking at home for two years at that point, and my family saw enough potential in me to let me have at it with the most important meal of the year. I loved juggling all the different parts of the traditional British Christmas meal, each being its own masterpiece: the turkey, the homemade cranberry sauce, the roasted vegetables. We also pulled Christmas crackers, which are cardboard tubes that you have to pull open with another person, and they make a loud bang, like a party popper. They look like a big piece of candy and are usually the size of a water bottle. Inside are a collection of small gifts, usually including a corny joke written on a piece of paper, and colorful paper hats. Then there was the Christmas pudding, which is like a rum- or brandy-infused fruit-and-nut cake, which you douse with more rum and light on fire. The fire burns up all the alcohol and caramelizes the outside of the cake before extinguishing itself. Every year we would crowd around the table after our turkey dinner, with our silly paper hats on, turn off the lights for added suspense, and watch the blue flames circle around the pudding faster and faster until it went out. I sat there at fourteen, "chuffed" as the Brits say, having served all those dishes at the same time perfect, hot, and from scratch, all without stressing for a second.

I'm still not sure how I really started cooking in the first place. One day, when I was twelve years old, I just decided to take over dinner for the day. I still don't know why or exactly when. Maybe I wanted a break from playing Hot Wheels with my brother all day. I don't even remember what I cooked. I didn't take cooking classes in school, but I knew the basics from my parents. I could cook pasta, a basic protein with a store-bought sauce like teriyaki, and a vegetable. Again, I still don't know how or why this happened; it just kind of did, but from then until I moved out at eighteen, I willingly cooked almost every family dinner.

I was still just experimenting and using whatever cookbooks we had in the house to learn. Cooking was never a stressful activity for me; if anything, it was stress relief. Along with Christmas dinners at fourteen, I started making silly cooking videos on the weekends. My brother would film and make silly noises in the background, and I would demonstrate some recipe I had found online, adding twists of humor. I was hustling at the age of sixteen, selling cooked dinners to my parents' coworkers and friends to raise money for my first mission trip to the Navajo indigenous land. I cooked curry for the Indian, sushi for the Japanese, and clam chowdah for the New Englander. They all raved about my creations.

Somehow I still didn't get the memo that I should be a chef. Throughout high school and college, I worked a few different jobs—mostly related to my love of snowboarding and my desire to work in the ski industry. I coached kids and was an overnight counselor at a summer snowboarding camp. I worked as a marketing manager for a local ski-related nonprofit. I had a full-time data-entry office job for *one* summer. Just one. Never again. Then I had that mountain ops job right out of college and planned on working at least another winter there. Finally, somewhere in the middle of wedding planning, in that whirlwind that was spring of 2018, I thought, *Heck, why not try cooking professionally, just for a summer? It can't hurt.*

Which brought me to the seafood spot.

RECIPE

A Very British Christmas Pudding

Although this is called "pudding," it is really more like a cake, and tastes of all things rum, spices, and fruit. It's now a tradition I've brought back and still do, even though I don't go back to the UK for Christmas anymore. This recipe was inspired by and adapted from the Rockrecipes blog.

Ingredients

2 cups raisins or mixed dried fruit
1/2 cup rum or brandy, plus more for the "flames"
1 cup chopped dates, measured after chopping (about 10 Medjool dates)
6 tablespoons butter, or suet if you want to go full-on old school
1/4 cup honey
1/4 cup chopped walnuts
1/2 cup brown sugar
3/4 cup water
1 egg
1 cup all-purpose flour
1/4 teaspoon baking soda
1/4 teaspoon baking powder

zest from 1 orange

small pinch of each: powdered ginger, ground cinnamon, allspice, ground nutmeg, ground cloves

Lighter, matches, or other fire source

Optional: 1 pound or dollar coin for the center

Method

The day before cooking, soak the raisins in the rum or brandy. Save at least two tablespoons for the flames, plus more for drinking. Combine butter, dates, sugar, honey, and water in a saucepan and simmer 10–15 minutes until you have a paste. Set aside to cool.

In another bowl, mix dry ingredients. When date mixture is cooled, add the egg, then mix it all with the dry ingredients. Then mix in the soaked raisins and the walnuts. Put it all in a greased, small cake tin or pudding basin/bowl/small bundt, whatever you have on hand. For a super-traditional pudding, put a (clean) pound coin or dollar coin in the center for good luck.

Bake in a preheated, 300-degree oven for 80 to 90 minutes, or until a toothpick comes out clean. Let it cool before removing from baking dish.

When it's time for the most exciting part of Christmas dinner and you are ready to serve the pudding, take the room-temperature pudding and put it on a large plate. Pour 4 tablespoons of the alcohol you used over the pudding, or enough so some pools around the pudding on the plate. Turn off the lights. Light the pudding on fire. There should be blue flames engulfing the pudding, circling around the plate where there is excess alcohol.

This should continue for a few minutes, until the alcohol is burned away.

Slice and serve with a creme anglaise or custard sauce if you want to make that.

CHAPTER 2

If You Can't Handle the Heat...

I naively walked into the short, purple building after seeing a Craigslist ad hiring line cooks, ready to talk about how much I loved cooking at home. Fishing net decorations and plastic lobsters lined the wall, and the pleasant smell of fresh seafood cooking made you forget you were in the mountains. I met with the owner and tried to flaunt the fact that I had been "a home chef for ten years," which was true, but I now know that means very little in a restaurant kitchen. Somehow, though, that was enough for them to hire me on the spot as a cook. I lived in a tourist town coming up on its busy season, so most restaurants were hiring anyone with a pulse who wouldn't no-call-no-show more than once a week. In this sort of environment, coupled with a housing crisis driving out locals, it seemed like anyone could get a job in a local restaurant kitchen. Still, few are successful in one. Just because it is easy to get in does not mean the work is easy. The reason a lot of restaurants "hire anyone with a pulse" is because the work is hard, and poorly paid at that, so few people apply and fewer people stay. I would soon learn that most restaurant kitchens are chronically understaffed. Many people start, then disappear a week later because it is too hard.

I found myself as the only woman in the seafood spot kitchen (weird, I thought the kitchen was "our place"), which I would later find out to be the standard across most restaurants. Based on their stories of past coworkers, I figured out I was probably the first woman to work the line in that kitchen. I didn't give it much thought. It wasn't something I had known would be the case coming in. I was just there doing my job. It was an open kitchen, so customers could watch you cook their food. I remember during one busy Saturday, a woman came up to pick up her food and said, "It's great to see some ladies holding it down in the kitchen!"

Being my first restaurant job, I hadn't thought of the kitchen as a male-dominated field. I just knew I liked cooking and wanted to give it a try.

Most restaurants have prep cooks and line cooks for each station, but this was such a small restaurant, everyone learned everything. In a bigger kitchen, prep cooks don't cook the meals to order but prepare foods like sauces, sliced cheese, or anything that wasn't made to order. A "line" in a restaurant kitchen refers to the place where the meals are cooked, so line cooks will, for example depending on the menu, grill meat and fish, put together salads and burgers, or work the stove range and ovens. If something takes less than fifteen minutes to cook, it was probably cooked to order by a line cook. If something is entirely from scratch or takes longer than fifteen minutes to cook, it was probably cooked beforehand by either the line cook setting up the station or by a prep cook.

Orders for a whole table usually come through a printer on a receipt-like paper and are put on a "rail" that holds the orders in a way the cooks can see them all in the order they were placed. A good team of line cooks will be able to keep track of every ticket on the rail at the same time, sometimes having more than fifteen up at once. (That's fifteen orders, not fifteen meals. If there's a table of ten, they still only take up one ticket.)

I started straight on the line. As a small kitchen, there were usually only one or two line cooks running the whole show. We would do most of the prep ourselves before service or between tickets. Quickly, I learned all the menu items by heart, and I became familiar with the ins and outs of working in a kitchen, so I was able to follow their recipes, prep, open, close, and work the line on my own.

The main guy who trained me was a toothless, middle-aged Australian man named Joe who said he had been fired from his last three jobs because of sexual harassment. (*but don't worry*, he says, *it was never actually his fault*).

Joe patiently taught me the basics of mise en place (although he didn't use fancy words like that), which is the basis of line cooking. Mise en place, or just "mise," means everything in its place. Fish-and-chips batter made before service? That's part of your mise. Tongs in just the right place? Mise. Gone to the bathroom and said your prayers before dinner service? Mise. Whether it's towels, sauces in squeeze bottles, or sliced tomatoes, everything is in arm's reach if you're working the line. If you're running off the line for garlic and chives, you've messed up.

Joe taught me how to grill diamond marks on fish and sear scallops to perfection. He went above and beyond in not only teaching me the menu items but how to do the absolute best job. Soggy fish and chips or overcooked scallops were apparently acceptable to some line cooks, but not to him. One day he caught me dumping lobster in a haste into a lobster grilled cheese. He stopped me right away.

"You're starting to cook like the guys here who don't give a shit," he said, moving around the pieces of lobster meat on the sandwich. "Every bite should have a piece of lobster. Don't let me catch you doing that again." I appreciated that he held me to high standards. I didn't see him do this to the other guys, probably because they thought they were better than him and didn't want to listen.

Here was this guy, with no formal cooking education, doing a wonderful job teaching me everything I needed to know about the basics of line cooking. Thanks to Joe, everyone was shocked at how quickly I learned to efficiently work the line, despite no experience or culinary school. I came in not even knowing what a Reuben was, and a week into the job, I was successfully working the line on my own.

Besides Joe, I worked mostly with a short, Hispanic guy my age named José and his cousin Eduardo. When I started on the line, José always made some snarky comment about how I shouldn't be there or how I did everything wrong. One day I made the mistake of crossing over to "his side" of the line to reach something, and he "accidentally" turned around at the wrong time, holding a hot grill spatula, and singed the back of my arm.

"That's why you don't cross over to my side of the line," he said unapologetically.

I didn't listen to him and kept my head down and worked. Line cooks don't have time for drama at 1 p.m. on a Saturday. After a few days of this, I was in the basement grabbing flour and condiment cups, when I saw the owner and head chef.

"So how do you like working the line?" asked the chef.

"I love it!" I said, "I think I'm starting to get the hang of all the menu items and working a line."

"The chef and I think you're doing a great job so far," said the owner.

"I'm pretty sure José doesn't think so," I said.

"Pshhh … José? Don't listen to him. His five-foot-four ass thinks he runs the place," said the owner. "You're doing great. That's not even considering this is your first cooking job. We're happy to have you here."

Even if you're doing the right thing, there will be voices trying to bring you down. Always find the voices worth listening to.

***

Two weeks into the job, it was time for my first rush—
my first time "in the weeds," my first ass-handing. It was
the weekend of July 4. It's one thing to know how to cook
all the menu items. It's another to have fifty of them on
order at once.

It started right out the gates at 11 a.m. *Who even wants
fish at this hour?* José and I were working the two-person
line while the chef butchered fish and made clam
chowder in the back. The tickets wouldn't stop, and so
many were large groups coming up to celebrate the good
ole U S of A. For the first time, I ran out of space on the
rail to hold tickets. I watched the string of tickets fold
over the back of the printer and start making its way to
the floor. And of course, with an open kitchen, I could
see all the hangry faces, some of them audacious enough
to come right up to me and ask where their clam
chowder was. *How could there possibly be so many people here?
Who are these people, and why do they keep ordering food?*
Everything around me faded, and all I could hear was
that damn printer, and all I could see were columns of
black and red ink glaring back at me.

The old saying goes, "How do you eat an elephant?
One bite at a time." For big, overwhelming tasks, you
should approach it one small step at a time, from
beginning to end. Well, in the kitchen, not only would
serving elephants get the health department to close you
down, but you absolutely cannot work that way. With a
rail full, taking tickets one at a time will cause people to
wait all day for their lunch.

You can't put the salmon on the grill and stand there
and wait for it to cook before starting the next item. You

have to put the salmon on the grill, drop fries, dredge shrimp, then sprint to the walk-in to deadlift a fifty-pound bucket of cut potatoes for fries. On your way back from the walk-in, you remember to turn the salmon for those perfect grill marks before dropping the dredged shrimp in the fryer, then you pull the next ticket out of the printer, only to realize it is attached to five more tickets you haven't even looked at. As you put those in one long string on the rail and promise yourself you'll get to them soon, you dip fish in batter, make three salads, and then suddenly remember you have to flip the salmon over, only to realize you forgot about the shrimp in the fryer, which are now overcooked, and you have to restart them. Then you turn around and collide with your coworker who didn't say "behind, hot!" and now you have a nasty burn on your arm, which should probably be iced, but you don't have time because you have to take that salmon off the grill before it passes that fine line between undercooked and dry-and-chewy. Now that the salmon is done, you redo the fried shrimp, prepare ten plates for that table of ten who have been waiting for half an hour, salt the fries, plate, and get that order out, only to continue working on the other twelve tickets that are already in progress.

Time is warped on the line. You think an order just came in, but they've actually been waiting over an hour for their food. That day, most people did wait that long. Somehow, in the blink of an eye, it was 3 p.m. I took the last ticket off the rail and slapped it down on the counter with the food for it. "That was the last ticket!" I exclaimed. The whole kitchen cheered. Then the printer sounded off again.

What. Was. That? I thought at the end of all the madness. *That was nuts! But I … liked it?*

I felt a mix of being beaten down yet triumphant at the same time. I didn't handle that rush perfectly. By the end of it, I was taking the tickets one at a time, my brain fried like the breaded clams on our appetizer menu. That lunch rush kicked my ass for sure, but somehow, I was amped up and ready to do it all over again.

I wonder if I'll actually be good at this one day. All I know is I really want to be!

After making it through that, José and I seemed to get along better, and eventually we found ourselves goofing around and singing random, made-up songs while still working hard and busting out tickets on time. I may not have killed my first rush, but maybe I gained some respect from him after not walking out that day. Perhaps he had seen too many people do that and didn't want to respect anyone until they earned it.

Through July and August, I stepped into work every Saturday and Sunday ready for a beating. Heck, sometimes I even got my ass kicked on a Tuesday if I was lucky. Part of me wondered if maybe, just maybe, cooking professionally wasn't something I was quite cut out for. Somehow, I would sometimes find myself sending out food that was simultaneously cold and overcooked at the same time. I often wanted to crawl inside the walk-in fridge and put a bucket over my head and disappear, but I didn't have time. I didn't even have time to pee. They say, "If you can't handle the heat, get out of the kitchen!" The "heat" not only refers to the physical heat (which can get intense, surrounded by grills and fire and whatnot), but the stress and the absolute chaos and mayhem that is a restaurant kitchen during a service rush. Most weekends, I found myself asking, *Can I handle the heat? Or should I just get out?*

***

One day during that time, a server came back into the kitchen and said, "Who made the fish and chips?"

I did it. I had made the fish and chips, even making the batter from scratch that morning. *Oh no, what did I screw up this time? They must be undercooked, or too salty, or the fries must be soggy, or maybe I forgot the tartar sauce.* Reluctantly, I admitted that I had made the fish and chips.

"They want to give compliments to the chef for the best fish and chips they have ever had!" she said.

This was a surprise to me. I never expected I could cook the best anything for anyone. I was just some home cook who decided she would give it a go in a professional kitchen, and here I was, actually doing an okay job.

Now it was time for my second holiday weekend as a restaurant cook. It was Labor Day weekend, Sunday night. The head chef had worked the morning shift and was on his way out, and so was José. I was left with two guys—one Romanian seasonal employee I had trained named Dimitri, and Eduardo, José's cousin who worked part time and had started close to when I did.

You know when a situation starts getting out of control, so you look to find an adult, but then you realize you are the adult? That's what it was like. As expected, people began pouring into the small seafood restaurant, and soon the line was out the door. But we had our game faces on. We thought we were prepared. Keyword: thought.

As I was finishing up making my sixth crab Louie, as well as a table of twelve's order, I heard Dimitri exclaim, "Ah! We are out of shreeeemps!"

He had to run to the back and get some more shrimp defrosting, because we hadn't even prepared any. Meanwhile, I used up the last piece of fish for fish and chips (our most popular dish), and had to grab the butcher's knife mid-rush and start cutting filets of haddock.

If we truly run out of something, we can eighty-six it. Here's some more restaurant-worker jargon for you. Eighty-sixing something means you're out of it. No one really knows why. It's just one of those terms that have been passed on from restaurant to restaurant. We can eighty-six some items, but we will not eighty-six fish and chips. *Not on my watch.* Eighty-six sanity? That'll happen sometimes.

The cashier came up to me and asked what the wait time would be so he could tell customers. I looked up at the rail. We had tickets out the wazoo. My brain said definitely at least forty-five minutes, but out of my mouth came, "I dunno, maybe twenty minutes or so?"

"Okay, twenty minutes. I'll let people know when they order," he said.

What did I just do? I thought as I continued cutting lettuce on the line because we had failed to prepare enough before the rush. Then, we ran out of batter for fish and chips, but good thing those are easy to make because we premeasure and prep the dry ingredients, and all we have to do is add beer. Well, we looked in the place

where we kept said prepped bags, and whaddaya know—
we didn't even have any of those! In a crazy, frantic rush,
Dimitri ran to dry storage and began collecting the
ingredients to make the batter completely from scratch.

"Not all heroes wear capes," I said as he returned to
the line with a fresh batch of fish-and-chips batter.
Meanwhile, Eduardo had to scramble downstairs because
we had run out of those little cups we used for condiments
and coleslaw. After running out of a few more items, it
seemed as if we had everything under control, despite the
ten uncalled tickets still hanging from the printer. That was
until I heard Dimitri yell, "We are out of shreeeemps!"

"Again?" I said, in disbelief.

"Yes!" he responded, his eyes wide with just as much
disbelief as mine.

You know that moment when a stressful situation
becomes a comedy? Like things are so out of hand, all
you can do is laugh and roll with it? That was us. At
around 7 p.m. on a holiday weekend evening, there we
were, laughing at ourselves for being completely and
utterly unprepared. As he ran back to the freezer to find
more shrimp, we continued working through the rest of
the tickets until the rail was almost empty.

Toward the end of the rush, as tickets began slowing
down and you could count the orders left on one hand, I
began looking at the time shown on the ticket (when the
order was placed), and comparing it to the time we sent it
out. Lo and behold, almost no one had waited longer
than twenty-five minutes for their food! The three of us
had overcome all odds and delivered what we promised
—not sacrificing time for quality or quality for time. I felt
alive, on a high almost, like I had reached some kind of

milestone in my two-and-a-half-month career as a restaurant cook. That night, I learned that although failing to prepare means preparing to fail, there's still a chance to pull through if you are able to think on your feet, handle pressure well, improvise, and most of all, find a little humor in it.

I guess if you can't handle the heat, stay there until you can.

CHAPTER 3

Empowered, One Saw at a Time

The winter following my time at the seafood spot, I decided I would go back to the ski resort job I worked the previous year—working on the park crew. At that time, I did not know if cooking was the path I wanted to take, so I decided to keep the seafood spot as a night job and go full time back to the ski resort for the winter. Some days, I left the house at 6 a.m. to work at the ski resort, then worked there until 5 p.m., only to go straight to the restaurant until 9 p.m. I loved my jobs and kept up with that schedule. I took pride in being able to do that. That's what you're supposed to do when you're twenty-one, right?

Early that winter, I was taking one of those crucial "mountain inspection" laps, and I ended up needing something from the shack at the top of the mountain.

"So, you're the girl from park crew," I heard a woman's voice say. I didn't hear many of those during my workday. I looked up and saw two ski patrollers. Ski patrol are those people with red jackets and the first aid cross who work as "ski ambulances" for injured people.

"Sure am," I replied.

"You're looking at about 50 percent of the women on ski patrol here," she said, pointing to herself and her coworker.

"You're looking at 100 percent of the women on park crew here," I said, pointing to my lonely self.

"Always remember, the guys will try to give you crap. Don't ever let the guys give you any of their crap," said the patroller.

I took a mental note.

Park crew was my job for that winter. At a ski resort, a park is a place where the resort builds jumps, halfpipes, rails, and other creative features that skiers and snowboarders ride on. If you watch the Winter Olympics, think of the halfpipe and slopestyle events. I was on the crew of people who built, tested, and maintained them at that resort. By *test*, I mean I actually rode on the features on the clock. We slid over rails and flew through the air off jumps. We made sure the halfpipe was riding just right.

Most of the features were built at night with Snowcats. Cats, or grooming machines, are these huge, half-million-dollar machines with a blade on the front and a tiller on the back that drive on the snow and can move huge piles of snow to create takeoffs, jumps, and even halfpipes. They also smooth out the snow surface every night, turning a beat-up, icy ski slope into fresh corduroy. As day crew, I did not drive these machines but did more of the fine-tuning and hand work, as well as daytime maintenance, since we couldn't drive the Cats on snow while there were guests on the hill. We were also responsible for all the rope lines, fences, and signs around the resort, and we had to shovel snow off all the features when we had a storm. We were often found loading and unloading the chairlift and riding down with tools, carrying fifty-pound buckets with us down the hill.

We saw the sunrise and the sunset in the same shift, and not just at the end of December either. There is always one week in mid-January where the peak of the sunrise would happen right as our crew arrived at the top of the mountain in our all-terrain ranger with snowmobile tracks instead of wheels. There we would be—me and a bunch of raunchy, hard-partying ski bums, marveling at the beauty of the way the sun turned both the sky and the snowy mountains a peachy pink.

My first season in that job was nothing but a blast. The winter right after graduating and right before I worked at the seafood spot, I wanted a fun, chill job for a season to see where to go next. I wanted to work at the ski resort where I had spent my college years riding. I applied for a few different on-mountain jobs. Ski patrol said my riding ability was up to par, but I didn't have the medical experience. Being a snowboard instructor seemed cool, but as soon as they asked about my experience with kids, I knew it wouldn't be a good fit. I had always watched the park crew at work and had thought it could be a pretty cool gig. I had never seen women work that job in all the ski resorts I had been to, but to me, that was never an issue. I hoped they wouldn't bring it up or make a point about it. They didn't. I was there to do the same job as the guys and expected to be held to the same standards. I wanted to be hired based on my work ethic and competency, not because they "needed diversity" or "wanted to show they were empowering women."

I stepped into the run-down, single-wide trailer of an office for my interview.

"Have a seat," said Chris, the main department boss.

I looked around. There wasn't one. All I saw were power tools and puppies.

"Here," said Ralph, the direct supervisor over the park crew day staff, flipping over an old paint bucket. I sat down.

Okay, this is pretty casual ... I like it.

We talked about my snowboarding experience, my willingness to work as a team, and how I hoped to give back to the park I loved to ride so much. I hadn't even finished the interview when I knew it would be a good fit. Apparently, they saw it too, and a few hours afterward, they told me I got the job.

My first season on park crew was so much fun, I knew I had to go back for seconds. Part of that decision was the awesome crew of people. This second year, I was the only woman in the entire department, rather than one of two my first year, but I had learned from the year before that working with guys was a blast! There had been no drama, tons of laughs, and lots of joking around while still working hard. We could turn an eleven-hour day of shoveling snow into a day of shovel racing and fun. The guys had my back, accepted me as one of them, and didn't make any special adaptations for me because I was "different." There were some new faces, and some I knew from the previous year, including the bosses.

Chris, the manager of the whole terrain parks department, was an expressive storyteller who would have the whole room howling with laughter a least once a day. He always had a humorous remark on deck, and there were times it took a little bit to figure out he was being sarcastic.

"I think they will give you coins," he said, when someone asked how we would receive our first paycheck, "in purple, velvet sacks, tied up with a golden rope. I don't know! How about we go to HR and find out?"

Ralph was the direct supervisor over the park crew day staff under Chris. He was six foot five, didn't have a bank account, and used a flip phone. (The year was 2018.) He said he met his girlfriend (equally tall) when "I pulled out my flip phone … and she pulled out her flip phone … and I knew."

Being a returner this season, they had some off-season work they would do in the fall before the snow fell, like clearing trees and maintaining and building the metal and wooden features that would be put in snow. I had zero experience with power tools, except for one time my dad showed me how to use a drill.

I showed up at my first day, eager to help. I wasn't sure what to expect, since all the guys there had been there most of the summer or had experience in similar jobs. First thing in the morning that first day, a coworker and I were putting some bolts in a new feature, and in an unfortunate turn of events, or just bad judgment on my part, his wrench ended up coming off the bolt and hitting me square in the face, and next thing I knew, there was blood all over my hands. Whoops. Way to start the season. Welcome back! After checking that all my teeth were still there, I cleaned up and started to wonder why I even thought starting this job was a good idea. I imagined my supervisors in the office looking outside and saying, "Why'd we hire *her?*"

Unlike the guys, I had no special skills in the field like welding or concrete-laying or big-machine driving, and now apparently, I had proven that I wasn't even capable of using a damn wrench.

The rest of that day, I mainly helped, held things in place, took measurements, those kinds of tasks, while I watched the guys do all the sawing, the welding, the driving of forklifts. At the end of the day, my lip still throbbing from the wrench incident earlier, I was standing around, looking for something to do, or at least something I knew I was capable of doing. I felt so useless. I was watching two coworkers use a bandsaw to cut long pieces of metal, when Ralph motioned me to come over.

I thought I was just going to watch or help guide the metal, but then he handed me the safety glasses, and stepped away from the bandsaw. With my hands on the controls, he showed me how to safely cut the metal. You want to make someone feel empowered? Let them learn by doing.

Over the next few days, my eyes were opened to just how many different kinds of saws there could be. I used a Skil saw, Sawzall, chainsaw, bandsaw, handsaw, pole saw. A common theme became one of the guys handing me a tool, like a chainsaw, then I'd have to tell them I'd never used one before, and they would teach me. It was no big deal. I never felt ridiculed or excluded because of my lack of knowledge. They didn't assume that I wouldn't want to use a Skil saw or a grinder and not even give me a chance. Maybe they'd never had to work with a woman before and didn't know what to do differently, so they treated me the same. I didn't want to be held to a different standard or given any special treatment, and they were giving me exactly what I wanted. I was becoming empowered, one saw at a time.

Out of all the saws, the chainsaw or pole saw was my favorite. There's just something special about going out into the woods and watching the blade melt through the tree trunks and branches. Pole saws are like chainsaws but with a smaller blade and on an extendable pole. We felled small trees in the ski runs and took branches off so they wouldn't whack people in the head when the snowpack made everyone fifteen feet taller. Another one of our supervisors, Scott, was a red-bearded, truck-driving, tobacco-chewing, large man who absolutely lit up when he had the privilege of passing on his passion for chainsawing to someone new. He gleefully showed me how to put gas and chain lube in the chainsaw, how to take apart the saw and adjust the tightness of the chain, and how to sharpen the blades on the chain. He taught me to start the choke, pull the cord, and run the saw.

"It can sense when the person using it isn't man enough," a coworker joked when one of the guys couldn't get the chainsaw to start.

I picked up the chainsaw and pulled the cord. It ran just fine. We all laughed, including the guy who couldn't start the saw. What is it with certain objects, like, say, a chainsaw, being considered "manly" anyway?

Being my second season, my goal was to grow beyond what I had been doing during my first season as a rookie and start leading and taking on more responsibilities. I liked the ski industry so far and wanted to see where I could take this job. This was one of my first full-time jobs, besides the seafood spot and high school and college gigs. I didn't know they were looking for another lead position alongside Ralph for the upcoming season. However, I noticed they had promoted another returner, Derek, who had started the year before like me. I tried not to make any assumptions on why they promoted him and not me, or more, why I had not been considered for or asked about the position. *Maybe, unlike me, he talked to them throughout the summer and specifically asked if they were hiring lead positions. Maybe he has more experience leading or just job experience in general.*

I think it can be easy to jump to conclusions about why certain people made it to certain places. We try to pinpoint the one aspect that makes us different, when really, it's not about that.

I brushed it off, thinking maybe I'd have an opportunity later in the season.

When the snow fell in late November and the resort opened for business, I met everyone else. We had such a fun crew again. A ski patroller who saw us from afar told us we looked like a circus. There were many moments, aside from Chris's humorous remarks or outrageous stories, where we would all be doubled over laughing. Once, the guys were passing around their phones on break to peruse Tinder. When one of my coworkers,

Dave, handed me his phone to look at this chick he thought was "posing" as a snowboarder, I started swiping left and right at random.

"Who knows," I said, "maybe I just set you up with your soul mate."

I didn't mind the stink of the unisex locker room/office at 6 p.m. after a twelve-hour shift, where we'd all take off our boots and compare whose feet were steamier (sometimes, I won that contest). Fifteen of us day staff and a few of the Cat-driving night staff (the people who drove the big machines on snow) would cram into that singlewide trailer at the evening shift crossover, along with all our skis and snowboards, all the office equipment, and enough power tools to make the Home Depot jealous. Often, one of us would bring beer, and we would sit there after a long day and share funny stories from the day, or joke about how sore we were from shoveling so much. Shared hardship is the best kind.

"It's like tennis elbow for poor people," said Chris, talking about a specific ache you get in your arms from the job.

There were so many running jokes our crew had with each other. One of them was about Scott hunting and skinning squirrels in his free time.

"Squirrel! Don't tell Scott!" we would shout whenever we spotted one.

Along with the thirty men in the terrain parks department, I also shared a break room and common area with almost the entire mountain ops department. This included the vehicle maintenance, chairlift maintenance, snowmaking, and grooming (like driving those big Cats to make the snow smooth) departments. That made me the only woman out of about sixty in my workplace. Those departments yielded quite a few interesting people too. There was Salty Steve from vehicle maintenance with a perpetual cigarette in his mouth, who used to work in the terrain parks department. According to Chris, he was so salty while building one of our wall-rides (a type of terrain park feature), we called it "Steve's Salty Wall Ride."

Almost every day, I was greeted by an overly enthusiastic, "Hey girl!" at six thirty in the morning, from one of our lift-maintenance guys. It wasn't creepy or a catcall. He just seemed way more excited than anyone should be at that hour.

My second season was starting off great. There was one day in December we had built a bigger jump, and like any feature, we had to test it in the morning. As we all rode down the run, we stopped above the jump, and one by one, the guys slid down and stood next to the jump to watch the tester. Next thing I knew, I was the last one standing up above the jump, and someone had to test it. With perfect form and speed, I pointed my snowboard down the hill, took enough speed into the takeoff, popped off the takeoff, sailed thirty or forty feet through the air with grace, and landed perfectly. Ever have those moments where you feel like you're representing your entire gender or group because you're the only one there? That's how I felt. And I felt like I was doing great.

Still cooking at the seafood spot at night, I was putting in back-to-back-to-back fifteen-hour days with ease. I was young, driven, and trying to find out what I wanted in a career. Even God took a day off, but I thought I didn't need one. So He gave me one. A few weeks actually, and not by choice.

The morning of December 17 started out just like any other day. We had our morning meeting at six forty-five, and Chris started us off by telling us a story about a former employee who had injured himself while urinating in the woods, to inform us that upper management was saying there were too many on-the-clock injuries this season, and we all better not screw up anytime soon. Before the season started, there was an initiative to decrease workplace injuries, especially for people like us who ski and ride on the clock, by having lessons on safe skiing and riding. That day, two coworkers and I would go to one of these safety lessons. We were stoked we could take an hour off actual work on the clock.

That afternoon, our lesson started great, and I was riding through the park. I wasn't even on a feature when it happened. I decided to pop a "nollie" trick on my board, which is where you spring off the front (or nose) of your board and land smoothly on your feet, but instead, I sprang way too hard and flew through the air Superman style, going over the front of my board into half a front flip.

I was about to laugh, pull myself off the ground, and brush the snow off, when I felt that familiar but horrible feeling that I had felt twice before in my left shoulder. It starts off as a not-so-painful, dull ache and almost a little confusing. I couldn't move it, and it was becoming more painful each time I tried. I knew it was fully dislocated.

This can't be too bad, right? Last time, it just popped back into place then didn't bother me for three years.

One coworker saw it happen and stopped to check on me. I told him the situation.

"Here's what we're going to do," I said. "I'm going to pop it back in, and we're going to pretend this never happened."

My plan was so brilliant, it couldn't possibly be foiled.

"Do you need patrol?" he asked, after a few more minutes of watching me using my other arm to try to wrench the dislocated one back in the socket.

"I'm fine. It's really not that bad," I said through gritted teeth. I was being honest. I really didn't think it was *that* bad at first. I was in denial, and maybe a little disoriented from the fall. However, the longer a joint is out, the more damage is done, and the more painful it becomes. I could feel the muscles stretching and the bones hitting together where they shouldn't.

I can't believe this actually happened. Can I press ctrl-Z on my life?

By this point, I knew I probably couldn't ride down the run, but the thought of having to call ski patrol at work, in uniform, on a run open to the public seemed worse than the injury itself. My shoulder hurt even more now, but my whole arm was becoming numb, and I couldn't move it at all.

The other coworker was at the bottom of the hill and had been waiting awhile, so he called on the radio.

"Hey, Hanalei, got a copy?" I heard over the radio.

"Um ... We're dealing with a—uhm ... situation here. Give us a minute," responded the coworker with me.

"Ten-four," he said.

Women are used to being told we're overreacting. We are told to be quiet and not to make a scene. I felt like I had to be the macho one in front of the guys. I really didn't think this could be that serious at first, which is why I stalled for half an hour asking random people to "put my detached arm back on my body" before my coworker finally convinced me to let him call ski patrol, since I couldn't ride down the rest of the run. (I promise, I tried.) Patrol arrived, and after asking him if he can just put the shoulder back in (legally, he couldn't), I reluctantly stepped in the sled.

"Do you need a hand?" patrol asked as I stepped in.

Trying to joke my way through the pain and seriousness of the situation, I told him, "Yeah, I only got one."

I had just ridden down a run in a sled called "Main Street" in my work uniform. *Embarrassed* doesn't cut it when I saw about ten of my coworkers waiting at the bottom.

"Do any of you know how to put a shoulder back in?" I asked them as one last-ditch effort to avoid the clinic.

"Dude! No, just go to the clinic!" one of them said, in disbelief that I thought there was any other option.

The pain was becoming progressively worse and was making me nauseated and dizzy by the time I arrived at the ski resort clinic. They asked me fifteen thousand questions about what happened, insurance, and worker's comp.

Why can't that wait until after they put it back in? I'm suffering over here!

Finally, they started the process of putting it back in. Turns out, I wasn't overreacting, and yes, going to the hospital was a good idea. What I thought could just be popped back into place ended up taking all three doctors in the clinic pinning me down and taking over twenty minutes of straight wrenching and pulling my body in in different directions to get it back in. I had refused all painkillers because the last time this had happened, it only took a second. Halfway through, they even offered to knock me out entirely. It was that bad. I just wanted it over with—no frills or medications. Finally, they inched it back in.

As I left the clinic in my new sling, I was fuming with anger. In one unfortunate hour, I had learned that everything can change in a moment. One move on my board—a tame move within my ability level gone wrong—had potentially destroyed my season of working the job I love so much. And it had to be at a damn safety meeting.

CHAPTER 4

Fed Up

I had no idea how long this injury would curb me for. Because the job was on snow, I would need a doctor's clearance to snowboard in order to go back to that job. It would be three weeks before I would even have my first assessment. I didn't know what I would do if I just had to lie there, when I was used to working seventy- to eighty-hour weeks. The uncertainty was hard. For a few days, I couldn't use my arm at all, but soon, I could use it enough to get by on my own—and to cook.

I had kept the seafood spot as a night job a few days a week. About a week after the incident, I told them I could temporarily return full-time until I was allowed to go back to the resort. It was one of the busiest times of the year for restaurants, so they gladly took me back. During the Christmas holiday season, I was back at the seafood spot, slinging lobster rolls and fish and chips again. At 5:30 p.m. on the day after Christmas, one of the main cooks decided he was "too good" for the place and walked out, leaving only me and Eduardo (the cook who was there for the "ran out of shreeeeeemps" Labor Day service). We were both experienced enough on the line to pull through while short a cook. We finished the holidays strong.

***

Three weeks after my injury, I was cleared to go back to the ski resort job. I was happy to return, but my time over the holidays at the restaurant had reinspired my love for cooking professionally full time. You'd think my injury and time to sit still a little more would have taught me to ditch the seventy-plus-hour work weeks. Instead, I went at it even harder. This was mainly because I couldn't choose a path. I saw the opportunity for leadership at the ski resort job, but I didn't want to let go of my nights at the seafood spot. I also had a third, part-time freelancing job, which was also putting a strain on me. Physically, I could keep up with that work schedule, but mentally, it was wearing on me.

As I continued keeping myself busy, a thought popped into my head that didn't seem like mine: *Do you need another injury?*

No, of course not, I thought. *I'm just fine.*

Upon returning, I noticed they had promoted another guy, Rick, to a lead. Rick was a good guy and deserved the promotion, but I felt like I was never told about promoting a lead, never asked, and never been given the opportunity, even though I had been performing well leading teams throughout the day. It was easy to go into emotions and come up with reasons they had seemingly been promoting people behind my back, but I had to remind myself that not everything is about the fact that I was the only woman in the department. I was disappointed because I didn't know whether they were still looking for another lead. *Did I return for nothing? Is there any opportunity at all for me here?* For a while I was frustrated, but I knew I could either mope around and see myself as a victim or get the facts straight and prove myself with my actions and ability to work the job, even if it meant I had to work harder than the guys.

One snowy day in February, I was stuck in the office with Chris, Scott, and a new guy, Matt. Matt jokingly introduced himself as "the king of sexual harassment" on his first day, when he came in and saw there was actually a woman in this department. He had his jokes but never anything that made me feel degraded, stereotyped, or threatened. Matt and I ended up getting along, despite others not liking him. He was sarcastic, heavily tattooed, and "ate cigarettes for lunch." He was someone who was actually there to do work, rather than milk the clock or do the bare minimum. We worked well together, and I think he was just misunderstood, as he didn't talk much to the other guys.

Snowed in at the office that day, everyone else had been sent home, and the resort had closed due to too much snow. I asked if there were more opportunities for me to take on more responsibilities and leadership. Turns out, there was. I wasn't promoted that day, but they did give me an opportunity. Maybe it was a test. They were open to me being a leader. It was now up to me. They gave me the task of making that week's schedule for the whole department. Eventually, the schedule became my job, and I thought I was doing a pretty good job at it, despite working with many flakes who you never knew would show up or not. It was now my job to call new hires to figure out their schedule, and it was my responsibility to make sure we had the right people each day. I confirmed or denied people's time-off requests. For some reason, everyone wanted Monday and Tuesday off, and we were often understaffed those days before I started making the schedule.

"Can I pleeeeeease have Monday/Tuesday off?" asked Dave, the one who was usually found swiping left or right on Tinder during his breaks.

"No," I said, "we're super short-staffed and need people those days." That was hard for me to say, but it would have been harder to make it through two severely understaffed shifts.

"But those are Katie's days off!" he said. Katie was a cute snowboard instructor Dave would always point out when we were working on hill. Had they actually talked? Nobody knew.

I decided I would keep this in mind while I made the next few schedules. It wasn't my job to bend to everyone's personal needs, but these were my guys, and I wanted the best for them. A few weeks later, after moving the schedule around a bit, I was able to give Dave a Tuesday off.

"Thank you soooooooo much!" Dave said when he saw the schedule. I smiled.

"Go get it, Dave!" the guys cheered.

While we worked on hill that Tuesday, we watched Dave ride around with Katie. We all grinned when we saw them on the chairlift together.

"How was it?" the guys asked the next day.

Dave paused for a second, then with a sigh, said, "She's married."

I learned who to count on and who we would be better off without. My eyes were opened to the number of people who would bail on a job by essentially disappearing. I learned it was better to wait to put out a schedule, than to post an incomplete one riddled with question marks and incorrect shifts.

As I started to show interest in being promoted rather than kicking back as "one of the bros," I started to receive some pushback from the guys. To add to it, we were having a record-breaking winter for heavy snowfall. It snowed thirty feet in February alone. As the crew responsible for shoveling all the features, everyone was growing weary of shoveling for ten hours a day.

"These are the seasons that separate the men from the boys," said one of the park crew veterans, talking about big winters like the one we were having.

I was doing the same work, surviving it, and keeping up, but I wasn't a man. Or a boy. *I hate stupid sayings like that.*

Most of the pushback was coming from Derek, who was already a lead. It was as if he felt threatened by my presence—a small-framed, twenty-one-year-old woman with little leading experience. I couldn't understand why he had a problem with me. I was never one to stir the pot or cause trouble, and suddenly I had someone who seemed to hate me. Every day it was something different. For example, Scott and Chris began giving me some authority to lead groups and make sure certain tasks were completed. I still didn't have a title or more pay, but it was their way of seeing how I was as a leader. They would put me with a few guys, then tell me I was responsible for making sure tasks are done throughout the day. I would catch Derek bossing around the people I was put with, essentially telling them to listen to him, not me.

It was degrading and infuriating, watching Derek tell the guys I was supposed to be leading to do something entirely different, even though I had planned out something for us to do. As a result, some of the guys started walking all over me and treating me like one of the rookies. Some of them would talk in a condescending way to me all the time and would redo my work after I had already done it when it was fine. If one of them had a question and I knew the actual answer and answered it, I'd get shut down with, "I asked him, not you!" Derek told me to stop asking Chris and Scott questions because I was supposed to report to him rather than bother upper management, even though I knew they were developing me as a lead and knew I wanted more opportunity. On another snowy day in February (there were a lot of those), I ended up about a few hundred yards away from the rest of the group, and Derek thought I was out of earshot.

"I can't believe they let *her* make the schedule!" he said. "She should not be in charge of anything!"

They caught up to me, and I acted like I hadn't heard a thing.

This was essentially my first full-time job and definitely would be my first promotion if I attained it. This was a situation I had never dealt with before. I talked to my parents about it. I talked to a mentor figure from my church who had been in similar situations. They all said I *had* to do something about it. My parents told me to go straight to HR. I didn't want to pull the card, even though it was my card to pull, and rightfully so. Maybe it was pride. Maybe it was because I wanted to be the "strong, independent woman who don't need no HR!" At the time, it was mainly because I felt as if I couldn't bring up enough solid evidence that it was about gender. That shouldn't have mattered. A bully is a bully. I felt shame as if I had failed as the only woman in the department. *Everything that is happening is my fault. It's because I don't have enough backbone. This is why there aren't any women in this field. It's because I can't handle it.* I felt as if going to HR and being bullied was a symbol of failure—a symbol of pulling the "gender card," the only advantage I had. *And forget being promoted. If I did, it would only be because they "needed diversity" and needed to show they "valued women" or some other BS like that. There's no way I was actually deserving of a promotion.*

Still, I decided I would give it one more shot.

I cut my hours at my seafood spot night job and stopped working doubles. I decided to put more energy into my main job and ask Chris and Scott again for a promotion. It was after we had closed down the mountain and were packing up. They'd even opened up a few beers. They pulled up a chair, and we talked for a while in an informal interview.

They asked me why I think I should be a lead and what I would do to make the department and the park better. We talked about what was good and bad now, and I brought up what I had already been doing to lead others but felt like I was getting no respect.

I brought up how I had been making the schedule for the past month and how it had been going well. I reminded them of the times I had been put in charge of a group for a day and had been able to make sure everything they asked to be done was done that day. I had been taking charge, showing them I was competent at not only the job itself, but finding those jobs to do, and either doing them or delegating them. I gave them constant feedback on ways the park and the department could be improved. They saw it too.

At the end of the conversation, Chris looked at Scott and said, "What do you think? Should we give 'er a shot?"

Scott nodded. I had just received my first promotion.

It was March 8—International Women's Day—but I doubt anyone in the department knew or gave a crap.

Being "one of the guys" in a department of thirty men was easy. All you had to do was be everyone's buddy while doing your job enough and bring cold beer sometimes. Trying to be a woman and a supervisor in that department? Now that's hard.

CHAPTER 5

Now What?

The next morning, as we all gathered for our 6:45 a.m. meeting, Chris gave the announcement that we had a new lead. I stood up. I was so nervous. Even with the title, I wondered if anyone would listen to me. I wanted to be everyone's buddy like I had in the past, but now it was different. Then one of the guys broke the tension. "I object!" he stood up and exclaimed.

Is this guy for real?

There was a moment of silence.

Then he followed up with, "Nah, I'm just joking!"

We all laughed. I finally felt a little back to normal. Everyone had been on edge from not seeing the sun for about a month. It hadn't snowed in five days, and things were literally starting to look a little brighter.

My first day as a lead was eventful, to say the least. I felt like I was screwing up left and right every single minute. Sometimes my crewmates would listen and sometimes they'd disappear. It was like herding squirrels. (Squirrels! Don't tell Scott!) Sometimes I'd tell them to do something, and they'd respond, "No, I will do this instead." I felt as if the guys had figured out I had no backbone and they could push me around as they pleased.

That same day, that one thing happened that no park crew or ski resort employee would ever want to happen. A kid on skis hit a jump, overshot the landing, hit his head and had a seizure, requiring a care-flight out in a helicopter. Scott called me over the radio and asked me to bring a metal shovel to the jump where it happened.

"What is it for?" I asked.

"Blood and vomit on the trail," he said, like it was no big deal.

Later that day, Matt asked me sarcastically, "How was your first day as a lead?"

It was a rhetorical question.

"Great!" I said, with two thumbs up and just as much sarcasm.

The next day was my day off, and as I always did, I rode the park I had spent all week working on. It was a beautiful, sunny day, and I was trying to get my mind off the previous day's events. I rode with my friend from church and ended up taking a few laps with some off-the-clock coworkers. My shoulder felt as if it had finally healed from my December injury, and I was starting to hit the jumps I used to hit pre-injury. Then I decided to take one more lap before the mountain closed, and I decided I'd hit the main park instead of the small one.

As I launched off the same jump the kid almost died on the day before, I had this horrible feeling that this wasn't going to end well.

They say it's not falling that hurts but hitting the ground. I'm here to tell you that I got hurt in the air. I swung my bad arm weirdly, and it popped right out. I later found out that I had dislocated it enough times that I had torn the part that keeps my arm in the socket. All it took was moving it at the wrong angle to dislocate it entirely. That didn't make it any less painful or difficult to put back in. History repeated itself, and I tried to put my arm back in, asked a few others if they could, and finally gave up and called patrol.

"Hey, I recognize you! Weren't you just here?" said the nurse as I was escorted to the ski clinic for the second time in three months. That wasn't as embarrassing as the fact that all my colleagues had seen it all go down from the chairlift.

"We should just start calling you Hurt-a-lei," joked Chris as I came into work the next day in my sling. Again. I was at the point where I could laugh about it. I mean, the ski clinic nurse knew me by name at this point. Of course, I wasn't going to do my normal on-snow duties, but I decided I'd make the most of it. I asked what other work I could do as a lead in the department. I continued making the schedule, and they taught me to do other office work like budgets and time and labor. Chris let me email people in his name to take some of the office workload off. One night, I sat in on a ride-along in a park

Cat at night, watching the night crew build jumps and groom the ski runs. I attended management meetings with the GM of the resort and the mountain ops manager. The injury became a blessing in disguise.

I also ran other errands, since I couldn't be on my snowboard. The guys sent me to drive to the Home Depot to buy a list of specific items. I'd never driven anything bigger than my Subaru Outback, yet they handed me the keys to the company F-250, assuming I would be able to drive it. When I returned with the goods, one of the guys came up to me and said, "Why don't you turn around and back the truck in so it's easier to unload?"

My heart sank. Driving, let alone backing up large vehicles was not my specialty.

"Are you sure?" I squeaked. "I mean it's fine here."

I know there are plenty of women out there who kick ass at driving big cars and maneuvering them into tight spots. Well, they picked the wrong woman for this task— or so I thought at the moment.

"Fine, I'll do it wearing my ski boots then!" he said.

I refused to be shown up by a dude in ski boots, so I said, "Never mind, I'll do it." All the guys stopped what they were doing and started watching me. I put the truck in reverse. I turned around where I could and started backing the truck through a narrow corridor of cars, heavy equipment, and unused park features.

This moment would define how they see my gender in this department for the future. I couldn't screw up. Or give up and let Ski Boots do it.

I did it! I didn't hit anything, and I maneuvered the back of the truck into the tight spot, so it was easy to unload everything.

Maybe I wasn't letting my whole gender down after all.

***

A week after my second injury, I was cleared to ride again and work, although I stayed entirely off testing park features for the rest of the season. I picked up right where I had left off my first day as a lead, and I was winging it and learning on the spot every day. Like I had expected, the promotion didn't magically make everyone listen, but it gave me the space to gain confidence in leading and learn my own style. Sometimes I wanted to go home and cry from the emotional labor of being a boss over people who didn't listen. There were days I felt as if everyone hated me and I was the biggest joke to ever grace the department. A woman leader? In mountain ops? Hahahaha! Now tell me another joke.

Every day, I fought against the lies and self-doubt that I knew weren't true. *What if they only promoted me because they needed diversity or to show they valued women? What if they lowered the standards for me because of gender? When will they find out I'm a fraud? Do they know I'm twenty-one and have no leadership experience?* I reminded myself that these were just feelings and that I did deserve to be where I was. Sometimes, I had good moments. I tried to hang on to the small successes, even if it was just one task I had my crew do and they actually listened to me.

There was still one more problem though: Derek.

I knew the Derek situation wouldn't go away on its own, even after my promotion. It was clear he didn't want me as a co-lead. Although we were now officially on equal levels as a supervisor, I was still receiving snarky comments and general disrespect from him. He would refuse to address me as a co-lead and would go out of his way to say anyone's name but mine if I were leading a group out on the hill. For example, if I were leading a crew with Bob and Jim, he'd radio, "Bob or Jim, got a copy?" Then he would talk to them, even though I was the other lead for the day. He saw me as a threat, and I still had no idea what I had done to deserve that. I wasn't even "replacing" him or competing with him for a position. We were now on the same level.

I brought it up to Chris and Scott. I was nervous; I didn't like confrontation. Part of me wanted to shove it all under the rug and just "put up with" the disrespect for the rest of the season, then disappear quietly and hope there wasn't another woman who would want to work in this field in the future. It was hard to bring it up. It would have been hard to continue putting up with it. I had to choose my hard option.

When I talked to them, it turned out that they had already noticed Derek's behavior and taken action.

"Derek said something about you the other day, and I was blown away by how rude and uncalled-for it was," said Chris. "I shut him down right away."

"Really, what did he say?" I responded, not surprised.

"I won't say it, but it was pretty bad," he said.

I wasn't offended, since I already knew what Derek thought of me. I had an imagination, and I had also heard what he said when he *thought* I couldn't hear him.

Being on the receiving end of being talked about behind my back made me realize how harmful it is to gossip and talk negatively about people when they're not there, even if it's true. I realized that a good leader will shut it down right away, because it causes division within a group or a department. This was a huge lesson I took with me as a leader, even beyond this job. I had learned in church that gossip was bad, but I often justified it because it was true, and seemingly harmless. I was guilty, even outside of work.

How can someone trust a leader who talks about someone behind their back in a way they'd never talk to that person's face? Even if my gossiping was with no ill intent and only for fun, I had to do better.

I was happy to know the main bosses were already on my side. I continued and told Chris some more of my struggles as a lead, a lot of them applicable to anyone in their first supervisor-type job, let alone as the lone woman of the department. I was honest about how much of a hard time I was having but that I was doing my best.

"Well, you know, this job is ..." He paused and thought about how he would word it, "like a construction job, or landscaping. And the kind of people who work it are ... the kind of people who work those jobs."

Just say it.

"Well, there aren't a lot of women, so that makes it ... harder," he said, sounding like he wasn't sure if that was taboo to say or not. It wasn't. For once I felt recognized— relieved that they understood that was one aspect that may have made it harder for me in my new leadership position. I always wondered what they thought about that. I felt like I pretty much blended in with the guys and did my best to do the same job and insist on being held to the same standards—even the physically demanding aspect, the long hours, and now having to lead.

"This is just, my first leadership job ever," I said, glad I had a space to be honest, "I mean, it's basically my first job I've had an opportunity like this."

"Remember, Scott and I promoted *you*," he said, "Not Bob or Dave or Jim. We promoted you because we believe in you and wouldn't have done so if we didn't."

I needed that. It wasn't an ego boost—it was a glimmer of hope. So they *didn't* only promote me because they needed diversity or to show they valued women. They *didn't* lower the standards for me because of gender. They *didn't* only promote me because they felt sorry for me. I was *not* a fraud. I was *not* the biggest joke to ever grace the department.

Derek seemed to back off after that. I was gaining more respect from the other guys over time, and I felt more confident in my role, knowing that the bosses had my back, believed in me, and were actively shutting down gossip and backstabbing. Yes, Derek still had his job as my co-lead. No, he didn't suddenly become my best friend. I learned that not everyone at work is going to be your friend, as much as I would love to be. I learned to forgive someone who had made my job so difficult for those few months.

***

For the first time in my life, I was learning my own leadership style. We can take a quiz, read a book on leadership, attend a lecture, or talk about it to try and find out our own style, but at the end of the day, I had to get out there and do it to really find out. Often, I learned through my own shortcomings and failures. *Okay, so that's not how you lead people.*

One principle I valued from the start was the idea of being a servant leader. Growing up with Christian values and beliefs, "servant leadership" was a phrase often thrown around within Christian circles. I had been taught, and still believe, that Jesus had come down to earth to serve rather than be served, and he modeled this by serving people while still being recognized and honored as a leader. This was my first chance at leadership and my first chance to live out this principle. I wanted to be the leader who would just do everything rather than boss everyone around. *Then I'll get people's respect.*

I was the worst delegator when I started. If I saw that something needed to be done—even something that was hard work like shoveling out a feature from under ten feet of snow, I would just do it, sometimes by myself (yes, even after my *second* busted shoulder). It seemed faster that way. Why would I ask someone to do something if I could just do it myself? It seemed lazy and egotistical. I had to learn that it wasn't.

The ongoing learning for me has been balancing servant leadership and delegating. While it is true that people will respect a leader more if they work hard and don't see themselves as "too good" for anything, it is also hard to gain respect as a leader if you don't have any authority. By "authority" I'm not talking about a title, I had that. I'm talking about actual respect from your peers. At the beginning, I felt it was easy for me to just be a doormat and let the guys push me around. Slowly, I gained confidence and began learning this balance. I found myself becoming comfortable with telling people what to do if I was going to be there next to them, doing it with them. I liked being able to lead by saying, "Let's …" instead of "you go do …" Have you ever had a boss who seemed to just sit at a desk and bark orders? How did you and other coworkers respond? Did you respect him or her as a leader?

When delegating or finding tasks to do together as a team, I had to be specific about what we were doing, not wishy-washy. No more, "I guess we should …" or "I guess we can … at some point …" or, "Hey, so, you wanna do …" I defaulted to those sorts of phrases because I wasn't used to having authority. That had to stop. I had to be sure we were doing what we were doing, and confident, and boy did I have to fake it for a while.

I learned too that, as a leader, you're held to a higher standard by everyone else. People watch your work. Can you perform the basic task at hand? If I made a small mistake, it wasn't just a small mistake. *Some leader*, they'd think if a ramp I built looked like crap. I could feel them scrutinizing my work. In a way, it's good for leaders to be kept in check like this, not just by the boss, but from the bottom up.

I let them have some fun if we had the time. I was allowed to. Sure, we had plenty to do during the eleven hours we were there, but we usually had time to take at least one fun lap. We worked at a ski resort, and most of us only wanted that job because we loved to ski and snowboard! Of course, work came first, but it was my job now to find that balance between keeping the guys happy and putting my foot down when we were going to work.

I joked with them, laughed with them, and even took my turn bringing cold beers for our after-work locker room party. I continued making the schedule, refining and tuning it each week to be the most effective.

The biggest change for me was having to take responsibility for others' actions if I was in charge. I had to find tasks for my crew to do, and if we were caught fooling around, it would be on me. Some days it was easy to find tasks, other days I had to search. If Bob, under my watch, did something he wasn't supposed to, that was on me. I was looking out for my bosses and the company, not just myself anymore.

This job—a small promotion to lead over a few entry-level workers at a manual-labor job seems insignificant in the long run, but for me at the time, it was an opportunity I will forever be grateful for. I had learned so much about leadership, teamwork, and life in general, all in a few short months, thanks to great bosses and a whole lot of trial and error. Never mind being the only woman in the department—if anything, that only made it all the more interesting.

***

One day during that time right after I was promoted, I was talking to Rick, the other lead, who was twenty-two, like me, and had started in the department the same year I had. Like me, he had been promoted midseason, during the time I was out for my first injury. He noted that he faced the same struggles of people not listening to him and going off into their own world.

"It's hard when you tell someone what to do and they don't want to do it," he said, "especially when you have some responsibility for other people's actions."

Wait—it wasn't just me? He faced the same struggles I did? So, it's not because I'm the only woman?

It wasn't about gender. It was about being a supervisor! That's just part of being promoted, male or female. I was relieved to find out I was not the only one who struggled in leadership, and that something I couldn't control, like gender, wasn't my roadblock. The men had also fought hard to be where they were. They faced struggles as a leader too.

I knew I wasn't the perfect leader. I didn't even know if I could consider myself a good leader. I felt as if all eyes were on me whenever I screwed something up, and someone always had to make a comment about it. When I actually found myself doing something right as a lead, I felt as if no one noticed. Because my style was more telling someone to do something in person and often completing the task with them, my work sometimes went unnoticed, whereas Derek would bark orders over the radio so the boss would hear everything he was delegating.

I ranted to Matt about this on a few chairlift rides one day. He was one of the few people I could trust with a rant. Not only was he on my side in the whole Derek situation, but he also mentioned how our boss, Chris, did see and notice what I was doing right. Matt had been calling Derek out before I had even talked to the bosses.

"Oh, he sees," said Matt. "He sees all of that. You're doing a great job as a lead. I've been telling Chris that. And I've also talked to him about Derek. Trust me, it seems like he is favoring Derek by sending him to all the management meetings, but it's probably because he would rather have you here on the mountain, leading the actual work."

Turns out the "king of sexual harassment" was actually my ally. Matt, a heavily tattooed chain smoker with all the dirty jokes, ended up being one of the main supporters of the department's female lead. Don't judge a book by its cover.

***

Although I was stretching, growing, and being challenged daily, I thoroughly enjoyed those last few months of my season there. March and April are always my favorite time of year. In spring, resorts are mostly full of locals who love to ride the park. The sun is out, the stoke is contagious, and there is still plenty of snow to slide on. The park is like one big spring break party. I loved working my butt off with the crew on the park in a T-shirt and giving high-fives all around. I didn't mind the extra work created by warm spring days and melting snow.

I wanted to make the most of my time with that specific group of guys. It wasn't all peachy and perfect, but I knew I was going to miss this group. Overall, they were such a unique, fun group.

Coworkers are an interesting concept. They're not your friends, but you probably spend more time with them than with any one of your friends. You don't choose them for the most part. You can meet such interesting people at a job, and you can know so much about each other and then never talk again when the job is over.

There was Corey, a book of knowledge with an eccentric personality. He seemed to know everything about everything and always had a random fact on deck for the perfect moment. When asked how tall he was, he responded, "Six-foot-three, the same height as Donald Trump, who is the third-tallest president in US history. Abraham Lincoln was six-foot-four."

There was a day in April when we literally spent the whole day digging a hole. But guess what? We had a blast.

Between the injuries, the drama, and the long hours, I could say I had a tough season. Looking back, I realized I wouldn't have had it any other way. And that spring, with the terrain park in full swing, the resort guests having a blast, and the park crew out there every day crushing it, I was happy to hear a whole lot of, "Nice work, boys!" with the occasional, "Oh, nice work, boys and girl!"

CHAPTER 6

Back to the Kitchen

When the ski season ended in May, I had to find a summer job. I liked the seafood spot, but I wanted something bigger—something that would help me find out if I *really* wanted to cook for a living. At this point in time, I was planning on returning to the ski resort job after one summer to continue improving my leadership skills in a position I had fought hard to earn.

I surveyed the streets of my little mountain town, trying to find a place where I could have my ass handed to me every day and truly push my own limits. There was one place, a casual but kind of swanky downtown restaurant which fit the bill. I walked in with my resumé, but they were busy and couldn't respond to me right away. I persisted and bugged them with phone calls for almost a month to schedule an interview. I had applied to a few other places, but I knew this restaurant was the one. It was the biggest restaurant in town, had a decent menu ranging from casual burgers to fancier, special-occasion entrees, and the line was always out the door. It was out of my price range though, so I had never actually been there.

Finally, I met with the chef, and I was able to talk about my year (well, one summer full-time and very part time during winter) of experience at my previous (and only) kitchen job at the local "seafood spot," saying I would love to learn everything I could at this place. I told him about my experience on both the line and in prep, and also my experience leading at the ski resort. I wanted to make sure he knew I was able to work a line. From what I had heard from other female cooks online, women often found themselves stuck in prep, salad, or pastry. Sometimes, they were able to prove themselves through years of hard work to land a spot on the hotline, all while watching their male colleagues be put straight on grill or sauté. I was determined to at least be given a chance on the hotline at this place, even if it was a big step up from the small mom-and-pop place I had come from.

"Yeah, I can handle the line. I can totally handle the line. I thrive off the rush. I was born ready for it. Molded by it. I am the Zen master. That's why I want to work here. It's always busy," I said, or something like that.

"Well, you'll definitely get that here," he said, "and you need to be able to stay on top."

The interview was less about specific cooking skills and more about my experience on a line, my desire to learn and grow in a job, and what the chef was looking for in an employee. I felt confident, like I could hold my own in this kitchen.

I just made it through a winter as a supervisor in a department of thirty men and myself. I've got this.

I somehow managed to dodge having to confess that I couldn't cook a steak to order to save my life, or that I'd never been to culinary school, or that I had absolutely no clue what "mirepoix" (a fancy word for celery, carrot, and onion) or "the five mother sauces" were. People told me I was a damn good home cook though, so I had that going for me.

I knew there were skills I lacked, but they were all teachable. Some skills, as I had learned from years of having coworkers, were not. I could work long hours in a physically demanding job. *Check.* I could work with a team. *Check.* I was reliable, on time, and valued integrity. *Check.* I had passion and loved cooking. *Check.*

"Can you start on Friday?" he said.

I showed up on Friday, eager to work and learn the long menu of everything from to fish tacos to filet mignon.

"Here, put this on," said the prep cook and only other female cook, throwing a white chef's coat and white apron my way. I had never worn one before. I thought they were only for famous chefs on TV.

What? I shouldn't be wearing this. I'm just an amateur—a home cook with a little experience who thinks she has a chance in this restaurant. They haven't even seen me cook yet.

I buttoned it up and walked upstairs out of the basement-slash-employee-room through the dining room into the kitchen. Luckily, we hadn't opened yet, so there were no customers to stare at me playing dress-up.

This place was a huge step up from the hole-in-the-wall seafood spot I had come from. It had two walk-in fridges and one walk-in freezer (plenty of room to go in and cry on a Saturday night), one main kitchen, and a pantry kitchen out front with a wood-burning pizza oven and salad station. Most food, like sauces, pizza dough, and salsas, were made from scratch, and meat was butchered in house.

The main line, separate from prep areas, was a U-shape created by a long cutting board for plating up, a flat-top griddle, a grill, two fryers, and two six-burner stove sets . Inside the U, there was an island, but not one of those cute, granite-topped home kitchen islands you see at your hostess-with-the-mostest friend's house. This one was stainless steel with a steam table and toaster on top, and refrigerated drawers holding all the mise (prepped food).

This time, there were actually prep cooks and line cooks. The kitchen, being much bigger, was split up more into stations. The menu was split between stations based on how an item is cooked. Normally, one or two people hold down the pantry and cook pizza and salads. In the main kitchen, one person calls tickets, works the flat-top, and plates up; another mainly grills and helps with plate-ups and fryer; and a third rocks the nighttime sauté station—which consists of the twelve stove burners and two ovens. For example, if you ordered a filet steak, the grill cook would grill it, the sauté cook would cook the sides, and the person calling tickets (aka the "Wheel") would often put it all together, including sauce and mashed potatoes (made daily by the nighttime sauté cook). If you ordered pan-seared sea bass with risotto, this was 100 percent done and plated up by the sauté cook. That's what happens on a fully staffed night, so the stations will change if, say, it's midweek and there are only two line cooks.

This restaurant was big enough to have a designated expediter. The expediter or "expo" stands at the expo window (or just "the window" or "the pass") which is the heat-lamped gateway between front of house and back of house. They act as the communication between both sides of the restaurant. A good expo will make or break a service. They let servers know when their food is up, stay in constant communication with both kitchens on what the next pickup is, and keep their eye on the time so we don't pass our fifteen-minute limit.

"Are you a busser? Food runner? Prep cook?" said the current dishwasher, upon seeing the fresh, new hire.

"No, she will be on the line, next to me," replied the cook who was training me that day.

A wide, intrigued grin crossed the dishwasher's face. She was a stout Mexican grandma who had seen it all at this restaurant. If a server put dishes in the wrong place, she would unapologetically soak them with the spray nozzle.

"Goooood luuuuuuck!" She laughed, like I was getting up off the bench for the underdog team going up against the world champion.

Oh boy, is it that crazy being a line cook here?

As the rookie, I was willing to humble myself and do whatever menial task they wanted me to do. The first task they had me do was hand-slice pickles on the mandolin—

a culinary death machine which is a flat frame with a sharp blade used for making thin slices. Anyone who has ever worked in a kitchen has cut themselves on a mandolin. It's a rite of passage. If you haven't, have you really worked in a kitchen? I got that out of the way and earned that rite of passage there on my first day. Luckily, it wasn't too bad, and I was able to wrap my finger up quickly and carry on prepping for opening.

The general manager of the restaurant walked in. "Are you our new prep cook?" he said.

I see a theme here. Have there not been any women on the line here before?

"I mean, I think I'll be mostly on the line," I said, unsure since it hadn't been made fully clear what I would be doing.

Way to go making your first impression. You don't even know what job you are here for.

At eleven, we opened for the day. I thought I'd begin on prep or just watching, but I was thrown straight to the wolves on the line. One order turned into three, turned into seven. I felt like I had dyslexia as soon as we had more than three orders at once. I had no idea where anything was or what goes with what, or heck—even how to organize the tickets on the rail. One of the other cooks, a crusty, old guy, without saying a word, kept giving me this look, which said, *What is this, your first day?*

I had no idea who did what, what was going on, or where anything was. Meanwhile, a server was telling me the bison burger for table thirty-two comes with aioli on the side. I snapped back, "That wasn't on the ticket," and she showed me the ticket, and yes, it did say aioli on the side, so I had to remake the whole burger.

By the end of that shift, I began to wonder why I ever thought it was a good idea to leave the comfort of the seafood spot—where I had every menu item on point and knew that kitchen better than my home kitchen (where few items actually have a place). I felt as if I had just talked myself up at the interview big time, using state-of-the-art trickery to make them believe that I, an inexperienced, quiet, young woman with zero culinary school and little experience could hold her own on the line at the busiest restaurant in town. What was I thinking?

***

Just like at the seafood spot, I was taken under the wing of another middle-aged man who, although misunderstood by many, taught me all the little details that helped mold me into a successful cook.

Ken was the stereotypical burnt-out cook who had been working at restaurants since the age of twelve, when he lived in Chicago. Trained by "old school" big-city chefs in the nineties, he could be temperamental sometimes but held it down on grill and sauté. Although Ken had been working in restaurants for forty years, you could tell he desperately wanted a way out. To him, it was almost all he knew. He often fantasized about starting up his own catering company, but of course, that takes money, so he couldn't leave. Instead, he passed on his vast knowledge to the nearest willing subject.

Ken taught me to brunoise an onion, how to make "the best mashed potatoes in the world," and how not to make life decisions. He even introduced me to the nighttime sauté station early on—the one station most people either didn't learn or took years to be trusted with. He held me to a high standard and made sure everything I cooked was nothing short of perfect. I appreciated that.

"These are the little things that will set you apart as a cook," he'd often say, chiffonading cilantro or tapping the extra flour off a jalapeno popper before dunking it in tempura batter. You could tell he loved to teach just as much as cook.

Like at the ski resort, the guys there had not worked with that many women, let alone, as they called me, a *religious* one and, accustomed to constant locker-room banter, didn't know what to expect from me. They found out from the beginning that I was a Christian and attended church every Sunday before coming in to work brunch.

I never asked them to, but they censored their language at the beginning just for me.

"Don't say that!" one of them said to another when I first started, after hearing a coarse joke, "there are ladies around!"

"I really don't mind," I said, and I meant it. "This isn't my first kitchen job!"

Once, at the beginning of my time there, I came out of the walk-in to hear the tail end of some vulgar story about what one of the cooks did last night in the Motel 6. Their faces changed immediately when they saw I was there, and they quickly stopped the story.

"You know, you guys don't have to censor yourselves around me," I told them, "but thanks for thinking about me."

After all, this wasn't my first all-male job or even my first kitchen job at that, and I had been to twelve years of public school. It wasn't my job to force my faith on them or police their language. As long as I didn't feel degraded, stereotyped, or threatened, I didn't have a problem with a little coarse humor. Still, I felt flattered and respected that they had thought of me, and it showed there was still some chivalry and goodness in the world. Even now, I still hear the normal dirty jokes and banter, but no vulgar, detailed stories about what happened last night at the Motel 6, and I appreciated that.

Although people have called me "church girl" and "Jesus Lady," I still am not afraid to work with a bunch of coarse-humored, partying, outcast-type people from all spiritual backgrounds and walks of life. Jesus says Christians should "be the light of the world," which, to us, means we shine the values and fruits of Christ, such as love, joy, peace, and patience. But how can I be a light that shines if I only surround myself with light? Jesus spent his life on earth, as recounted by historically backed text, hanging out with the sinners, prostitutes, and those deemed "unclean" by religious folks. He had a construction job, and his closest friends were run-of-the-mill, commercial fishermen. Why should I do anything different?

I opened my ears and mind to learning from everyone, including Chad. When we worked our first service together, I told him I had already worked the line at a different restaurant. That didn't stop him from explaining to me how orders came out of the printer and how to put the ticket on the rail. He would move my plate one inch to the right because I had put it in the "wrong place." He'd say, "Don't do it that way, do it this way!" and then proceed to do almost exactly the same thing that produced the same result as intended. If you weren't doing everything exactly his way, you were wrong. The way my tickets were on the rail? Wrong. The way I melted the cheese on a cheesesteak? Wrong. He'd come into my station and start doing my job for me, even if I was not falling behind. He exercised all my self-control and patience muscles. I seemed calm, but I wanted nothing more than to tell him to *"get the *choice word* outta my station, man!"*

Instead of talking back, I decided to take a different strategy. I'd silently continue doing my job, then when he'd explain to me how, "next, you have to toast the bun for the burger," I'd say, "nope, burger is already in the window." I would cook circles around him, so by the time he'd try to take over my station for me, I'd be ten steps ahead of him. One day, after several instances of him trying to "help me," and me telling him I had already done it, he backed off.

"Okay, I'll just let you do your job then!" he said, both hands in the air.

Once I filtered out the useless mansplaining from Chad, I actually learned some new skills from him. Most of my knife skills I have today I attribute to Chad.

"See this?" he'd say about my large, uneven cuts along the wrong side of the onion, "That's home-cook shit. People come to the restaurant for something they can't do at home. They don't want the same knifework they can do themselves." He was right.

Although it was probably an ego boost for him, I let him show me the correct way to hold the knife, hold my noncutting hand, and get thin, even slices. I was open to humbling myself as the newbie and learning from everyone, even the ones I may not have liked so much.

Then there was Trevor, the fishing, dog-loving, kitchen lead who never missed an opportunity for a dick joke. He ran the grill and did most of the butchering when I first came on.

"This is the kind of food that will get you laid if you cook it," he said to one of the guys about our braised short rib dish.

On my second day working there, he asked me, "Do you even talk?"

"Oh, just give it a few weeks," I responded, smiling. I was right. Once I settled in, I wouldn't shut up. That's typically how I am when entering any new environment.

Trevor and I would have long conversations while working Tuesday nights together about religion and politics. He had grown up going to a private Christian school and had been put off "religion" by crazy nuns and strict rules. He said there was a lot of hypocrisy in the church, and that he had officially renounced his faith years ago. Somehow, he would still start conversations with me about faith. I just listened and understood, occasionally giving my two cents about my own experience in a less rigid, nondenominational church. As for politics, we both agreed the American political system was messed up and needed a complete overhaul. His dream was to somehow overthrow the central bank and become a martyr for the country if he were locked up because of it.

Ernesto was the main nighttime sauté cook, who kept to himself and was a man of mystery. He'd stand in the corner and sharpen his knife, and we all agreed that if everyone in the restaurant were to fight to the death, Ernesto would come out on top. He spoke great English, but the only noises you'd hear from him were silly, Mario Bro-like noises. He was always five steps ahead of the game. I worked many services, just me and him, and whenever I thought he was dragging something, it was probably already in the window.

Our chef, who hired me, was young for an executive chef and was much calmer than those executive chefs you see on TV or in movies. In addition to the ordering, scheduling, and office work, he was often found on the line next to us, running the wheel or busting out prep. He strongly believed in positive reinforcements and was quick to tell someone they were doing a great job.

"I'm not mad at you. I'm just teaching you the right way now, so you know," he'd say.

Gone are the days of screaming, condescending executive chefs being the norm. Cooks haven't become "softer" or "unable to tolerate what cooks used to be able to." They've become smarter, with more respect for themselves and less tolerance for disrespect as human beings. Our industry isn't perfect, but it's moving in the right direction.

CHAPTER 7

High Steaks

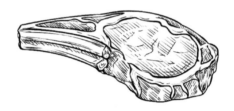

I was loving my new workplace and all the people in it and feeling more confident each day, but I still had my doubts. I knew my actual cooking skills needed some work, and I decided I would be up front about everything I didn't know. The guys appreciated my honesty and willingly taught me anything I asked, just like the guys at the ski resort with the saws. One of the main skills I needed to learn was steak. I took initiative and made it clear from the start that this was something I wanted to learn.

"Don't worry, we'll have you grilling in no time," Trevor said.

After mainly watching Ken and Trevor work grill for a few weeks, they handed me a thermometer, gave me a quick rundown on temperatures, and let me have at it. Had I decided instead to puff up my ego and lie about my skills, I may have screwed up a fifty-dollar steak on my first day, and my story could have been different.

Cue July 4 week. I knew enough on grill to hold down a "normal" dinner service. Chad had quit without notice. Unlike some other office jobs, when one person leaves, you can't just "pick up their work later." Whether there's two cooks or four, when that dining room fills up, we still better put out perfect food. Every time. Every order.

So, there I was—me and mysterious Ernesto holding down the entire main line while the July 4 week crowds flocked to our area by the tens of thousands like an angry mob.

I've heard too many restaurant workers say, "People can't tell the difference between med-rare and med-well anyway. Just put more sauce on it."

Or "Most people want their fish overcooked."

I call BS.

If you've ever paid for food at a restaurant that wasn't up to par, I am sorry, and I mean that. I'm not just screwing up your dinner. I'm screwing up your anniversary date night you saved up every penny for, your graduation party, or your night out with the guys. To me, it's more than food.

I am not a perfectionist in most areas of my life, but if a customer orders a medium steak, you better believe I want it to be perfect. This particular night, we were so swamped and understaffed, I was sending out food that made me embarrassed to leave the kitchen in uniform, in case someone put two and two together and muttered, "Hey look, there's the unqualified schmuck who messed up our dinner!"

That night, slightly burnt but passable sliders, burgers ordered medium that were a solid med-well, and charred buns left the kitchen while one member of a party of eight watched their group eat and sat without food because the kitchen misread their ticket. To top the evening off, the manager came back in and slapped down a cut-in-half filet mignon I had just sent out.

"They ordered this medium."

With no defense, I slunk my way back to the grill and put the steak back on.

The next day, I was back at work. The entire town was ramping up each day as we neared the Fourth of July. I began prepping for service—cutting and roasting parsnips, reducing demiglace sauces, and saying my final prayers that I would keep my sanity before the hungry masses arrived. Somehow, I ended up on grill again. Dinner service was busy, but it seemed to be running smoothly, until a server came back to the kitchen and said, with no particular emotion in his voice, "Who's cooking steaks tonight?"

The whole kitchen silenced, and all eyes were on me. My heart sank as I stepped away from the grill and hid my tongs.

I knew it—the steaks are going out wrong. They're all wrong! Do they know how little experience I have? I'm one of those home cooks who thinks they're all that but can't hold it down in a restaurant kitchen. This is it. This is the moment they find out I'm a fraud.

When the server saw who was responsible, he continued. "A man on table 11 who ordered the med-rare filet mignon told me to go to the chef right away and tell them he just had the best steak he's ever had in his life!"

I blushed, or maybe I was just red from the heat of the kitchen, standing next to the grill for five hours. Or both. I had the biggest smile for the rest of my shift, as we continued to work in harmony and encourage each other while we crushed the rest of dinner service.

"Did you hear that?" said Trevor, just as stoked as I was.

"Best steak in their life, Hanalei!" said Ken, doing a little dance while plating up orders on sauté.

I encourage everyone to give their compliments to the chef if the food was great. Maybe they'll just stroke an ego. Or maybe there's a struggling line cook out there, desperate for a sign that they are in the right profession.

***

In about a month, I had gone from not being able to identify a filet from a rib-eye, let alone cook either one of those to an ordered temperature, to becoming the main nighttime grill cook at the busiest restaurant in my town. Eventually, I didn't even need the thermometer anymore.

"It's like having X-ray vision," said Ken, pointing two fingers at his eyes, then toward the filet on the grill. He was right.

I would crank out huge tables of filets, rib-eyes, prime rib, and New York strip with no send-backs all night. This wasn't always the case. At the beginning, I had about one send-back a day, always undercooked. The British grandma in me hated cooking any steak over medium rare, but I did it anyway. Eventually I grew to be okay with cooking well-done steaks. It took off the pressure on those slamming nights when I was busy and couldn't watch the grill like a hawk.

Once I worked grill for a while, I learned that the servers were calling me the "Steak Lady" and were telling their tables that they could order a steak and it would be guaranteed to be just how they ordered it. I was flattered.

"Yeah, we have the steak whisperer behind the grill tonight. You should order the rib-eye," they would say. That medium-rare filet was not the last time I heard the "best steak" compliment.

A server told me once, "I love when a customer says, 'The steak was perfect. Tell the chef he did a great job,' and I get to say, sure, I'll let *her* know!"

Just as I had expected, some skills are teachable to a person who wants to learn. I would encourage employers in certain fields to consider factors beyond past experience and skill sets. Consider their work ethic, passion, and teachability.

***

At the end of that summer, I faced a decision. I thought I had already decided I was returning to the ski resort to continue gaining leadership experience. In the kitchen, I was still at the bottom. I could either go back to the ski resort and lead or stay at a place where I currently had no authority, in hopes of progressing. I had to make this decision before I left for surgery in August, because once I would return from my three-month leave, it would be the beginning of ski season. The surgery was to fix the shoulder I had dislocated too many times, and I would have to essentially not use my arm for three months, which would be a slight problem working in a kitchen.

I was waiting for one exact moment to confirm my calling. There wasn't one. I wanted one a-ha moment I could tell people if they asked, "So why the kitchen?" It's like how you know you're going to marry someone or how you decide on a certain faith. For some people, it is pinpointed to a specific moment. For others, it's a gradual process, but somehow, you find yourself sure you're sure. I was willing to give up the position at the ski resort I had fought so hard to earn and trade it for *potential* opportunity. I had to remind myself that fighting for the promotion wasn't in vain because with it, I gained experience, learned many lessons, and had a good time.

By the end of that summer, I knew I had to get back to the kitchen.

RECIPE

Coconut Braised Short Ribs

This was the first special that Chef ever let me run at the swanky downtown restaurant. He let me have full creative rein in the kitchen for the first time, so this recipe will always have a special place in my kitchen. Inspired by my Burmese grandma's recipe, I was able to adapt it and elevate it to restaurant quality.

Ingredients

4 pounds bone-in short ribs, or 2 pounds boneless "beef stew" cubes or cubed beef chuck. (This recipe works great with lamb too!)

1 14-ounce can full-fat coconut milk or cream

a few cloves of garlic, minced, or however many your heart tells you

1 thumb-sized piece/knob of ginger, minced

2 yellow onions

all-purpose flour, just enough to coat the beef. If you need to make this gluten free, you can use a substitute flour.

Salt, pepper

1 tablespoon turmeric

1 tablespoon cumin

beef stock or water—a few cups or enough to coat all the meat

4 bay leaves

Method

Preheat oven to 300°F. Alternatively, you can use a slow cooker. Coat beef cubes or short ribs in flour seasoned with salt and pepper.

Heat a cast iron pan or other pan that handles high heat until a drop of water sizzles on it. Add oil and sear off the beef until it has a nice sear on all sides. Clean out the pan after every few if the flour starts burning. Set meat aside in a Dutch oven, roasting tray, or whatever you would use to braise something in the oven.

Using the same pan (or a different one if it is too shallow or small for liquids), sauté the onion, garlic, and minced ginger until slightly browned. Then, add 1 cup water, the spices, and the bay leaves. Then add half the can of coconut milk. Save the rest for the end of the recipe. Heat in pan until boiling.

Pour braising liquid over meat. Top off with hot water so all the meat is covered.

Let it braise in the oven for four hours, or for eight hours in slow cooker on low.

Once meat is done, it should fall apart easily with a fork. If not, it needs longer. Put it back in until it is ready. While waiting, prepare sides you want. Rice or lentils are great for soaking up all the sauce!

To finish the sauce, set aside a few cups of the braising liquid. Add the other half of the can of coconut milk. Reduce in a pot on low until sauce is thick enough to coat the back of a spoon. Strain sauce through a sieve or chinois. Serve the sauce over the meat and sides.

CHAPTER 8

Surrounded by Sausages

In July, soon after starting at the swanky downtown restaurant, now working only forty to fifty hours a week, I somehow ended up with another part-time job on the side. I was not looking for another job. I knew the hours I had worked that winter were not sustainable, and I was striving toward not filling every second with work. But when I came across the post online from the butcher shop, I found myself typing up a response to the post and sending in my resumé. Next thing I knew, I was at the interview, telling them about how I would work for them from 9 a.m. to 3 p.m., then be off in time to go to the restaurant from 3 p.m. to midnight. Next-next thing I knew, I was breaking down tenderloins, sawing bone-in pork chops (another saw to add to my list), and fake-laughing at the front counter when a customer would say, "I'm a vegan, am I in the right place?"

The only other woman there at the time was the owner, though people still called her the "owner's wife." (Her husband worked somewhere else and had almost nothing to do with the shop.) She was pregnant when I started, and there was a running joke that she would name her son "Angus Prime." As a small business, the owners were very involved. I saw her at the shop the day before giving birth, then again only a week later.

The job at the butcher shop became my saving grace after my shoulder surgery in August, since the restaurant would not let me back to the fast-paced environment until I was cleared 100 percent. While in the bulky, post-surgery immobilizer, I worked the front counter, and when I was out of that, I started cutting meat again. I worked almost full time at the shop through October that year. During that time, I learned the true meaning of "God will provide." I was only able to pick up fifteen to thirty hours a week at the shop. Somehow, we never missed a bill or payment, thanks to money coming from the most random places. I survived on a carnivorous diet for a few months, taking home meats that were perfectly fine but too old to sell. Slowly, I was learning that working eighty hours a week was not the only way to live.

One day at the butcher shop, I was somehow trusted to run the front counter by myself while the others prepped in the back. I had learned quite a bit since I had started a few months back but was by no means a master butcher. Then a customer and her friend walked in.

"I would like a beef tenderloin roast, about one and a half pounds," she said, excited about whatever dinner plans she had made.

Easy, I thought. I'd taken apart enough tenderloins at this point. You find the "chain," which is a smaller, gristle-filled muscle that runs along the side of the tenderloin, and use your fingers to separate it from the main muscle. That's most of what butchering is, finding "seams" in the muscles and separating them, rather than cutting flesh apart at random. You use a sharp filet knife to fully separate the chain, then put it aside for ground beef. Then you can pull off some of the weird membranes and fat with your hands, then cut off all the "silver skin" with the knife. Then it's ready to cut, either into steak or a roast, just like the one this customer had asked for.

Then she followed up with, "But butterflied flat so I can stuff it and roll it up."

Plot twist. This definitely is not a job for me, the newbie.

I had seen my boss do it once before, but he wasn't there, and I knew it was more of a "master butcher" kind of task. You just take the knife and kind of go *woosh!* And there, what was once a log is now a flat square of meat.

"Hold on a second," I said as I scurried to the back to get someone more qualified. The boss wasn't there, but surely at least one of the other guys would know how to do it.

"I'm pretty sure you just take the knife and go woosh! But yeah, I haven't done it either," they said. It seemed as if they thought none of them were any more qualified than me to do the deed.

No more enlightened than I was before disappearing to the back, I returned to the front counter, where, of course, the customers were watching, ready for the professional who knew exactly what she was doing to prepare their thirty-seven-dollar-a-pound filet. I tried to pretend I hadn't just disappeared off to ask someone how the heck do you do this.

I knew I couldn't just sit there and stare at the filet any longer. Sooner or later, they'd figure out that the person behind the counter was highly unqualified for the job. I took a deep breath and plunged the knife into the tenderloin.

Everyone in the shop watched as the master butcher made precision cuts. Little did they know that behind the counter was a clueless young girl who had, about a minute ago, considered going onto YouTube and typing in, "how to butterfly a tenderloin," but didn't because it would have taken too long. So there she was, just taking her best guess.

And next thing I knew, the log was now a flat piece of meat. It wasn't perfectly smooth like that one time I had seen my boss do it, but to my amateur eyes, it was close enough.

I walked over to the customer and held out the flat piece of meat.

"How does this look?" I said, wincing.

Her face lit up, "That's so beautiful! Where did you learn to do that?"

"Oh, you know, the owner showed me a while back," I half-lied.

Pleased with the filet, she paid and left, and that's when I realized that what I had just done was pretty much a metaphor of what adulting really is.

When you're a kid or a teen, you think that adults have it figured out—that they take every step knowing what they are doing and are trained professionally in their field. But as you grow up, you have a lot more "they didn't teach this in school!" moments, and you realize you just have to wing whatever you're doing.

Isn't that what adulting is all about?

***

In November, I was finally cleared to go back to work after surgery. Returning to the restaurant after three months off helped me realize how much I missed it and helped confirm my decision to stay. The butcher shop was fun and something different, but not as fast-paced as working the line through a rush. I also returned to the restaurant with a new set of skills after working at the butcher shop for those three months. I could now cut all our steak and trim up any other meats we needed. I could talk with confidence about where different cuts came from on an animal and the best uses for different cuts.

One lesson I started to learn after having a major surgery, was learning to ask for help. I could have gone back sooner, but apparently I had a track record of refusing to ask for help, and the managers agreed I shouldn't be able to return until I was 100 percent healed. Eager to get back to my job as soon as possible, I asked the general manager if I could return with the restrictions my doctor had placed on me.

"I'll just ask people to help me with anything I can't do," I said.

"But you don't," he said.

He had a point.

When they finally let me back, I was still weak, and I couldn't reach my arm above my head, let alone grab anything off the high shelves. I was no longer the chick who could unload fifty pounds of prime rib from a raging-hot oven on Friday and Saturday nights. It was one of my favorite moments every week.

"You need help with that?" one of the guys would always ask when I opened the oven with the prime rib.

"No," I'd say proudly as I kicked the oven door shut with one foot and slapped the hunk of perfectly medium-rare meat down on the counter. I was going to be off of doing that for a while.

As one of the only women in most of my workplaces so far, asking for help was basically taboo to me. I thought, to prove myself equal as a woman in these fields meant I wouldn't need to be a burden, always asking for help. *Equal and capable* meant I could do anything by myself, right?

Asking others for help not only benefits yourself but is also an opportunity to let others shine. It only took two bad injuries and a major surgery for me to learn. Hopefully, you'll learn the easy way, say, by reading about it in a book.

CHAPTER 9

The Most Wonderful Time of the Year

"You'll never guess what just happened," said Ken one day in mid-December. "I've been entering these online sweepstakes, and I just won 5.6 million dollars!" There wasn't a shadow of a doubt in his mind as he told every single employee in that restaurant the news.

Since Ken had taught me most of what I knew about cooking at that point, I kind of looked up to him. I pulled him aside. "Are you like, sure this is legit?" I asked, already knowing the answer and trying to make him see it. I had seen many spam emails telling me the same thing. If they all were true, I'd have enough money to overthrow the central bank with Trevor and buy out the whole establishment I worked for, giving out free prime rib on Fridays.

"I have the emails," he said, pulling out his phone, "It's all real, look! I'm in the finals. I've also won a flat-screen TV and a new iPhone."

He had a whole list of emails, almost as if he had one for every sweepstakes he had signed up for. They were all in caps, stating: DON'T PANIC! STAY CALM AND READ THIS! Or PLEASE DON'T DELETE. This wasn't fishy—this was a dumpster fire in the trash bin behind the seafood restaurant.

"I can't believe you think I'm lying," he'd say whenever I didn't seem fully convinced. I didn't think he was lying. I thought he was being lied to. We all believed that *he* believed.

Despite his "winnings," Ken still came to work that day and the next.

"I forgot to clock in today, but don't even worry about it," he said one day.

For about a week, he told and retold the story over and over until everyone was sick of hearing it yet again.

"Same story, Hanalei," our dishwasher would say every time he listened to Ken tell me the story again.

Ken began dreaming of what he would do with the money. He told me he would donate about a hundred thousand to my church. He told another cook he would buy him a Toyota Tacoma.

"I'll buy a restaurant, and you can come work for me as the sous chef," he'd tell me, which, honestly would be kind of cool with the way Ken and I worked so well together. I just wouldn't want him in charge of, you know, the finances or personal information or anything.

Then, three days before Christmas, our little mountain town ramping up for the busiest time of the year, he just —disappeared. Apparently, he was texting screenshots of his bank account to Chef at 3 a.m., claiming he had made it through the finals in this sweepstake and had officially won the prize. He had left his mandolin there.

"I'm sure he has the money to buy another one," we joked.

I had learned so many new cooking skills from Ken, and he didn't have to teach me any of it. He could have taught me to flip burgers and left it at that—keeping all the knowledge to himself so he would have that edge over everyone else. From him, I also learned that all kinds of teachers will come and go through our lives at the right time. We can be open to learning from any kind of person, whether it's a successful, trained chef at a culinary academy, or an eccentric, burnt-out cook who falls for an email scam.

I wanted it to be true for him, but I knew it wasn't. He so desperately wanted a way out of the industry he had been in for over forty years that he was willing to believe anything.

Ken was supposed to work that night, leaving me and Ernesto yet again to fend for ourselves while the printer spat streams of tickets our way.

"It's Sunday night, you'll be fine," said the day crew as they left. We were not fine. That day was the closest I ever came to smashing plates and walking out. I did rip apart and throw a chicken sandwich bun across the kitchen, after putting mayonnaise on it when the ticket said "No Mayo." When you're a restaurant cook in the middle of the dinner rush, you want to switch into autopilot mode. It's the only way you will avoid a slow and painful death by tickets. In autopilot, you're in a state where everything flows smoothly from one movement to another. Someone orders a bison burger. You put the burger on the grill. You toast the bun, then spread aioli on it, put lettuce, tomato, bacon, and grilled onion. Then when the burger is done, you put cheese on and put it on the prepared bun setup, and boom, in the window in one fluid set of movements that doesn't require you to look up at the rail. Even what seems like a small modification can throw a wrench in a line cook's flow. Imagine looking at a rail full of tickets, having to bend your brain around each person's special requests. One rib-eye orderer wants it medium-rare with no mashed potatoes and the demiglace sauce on the side. Another rib-eye orderer wants medium, but no asparagus. One of the medium-rare bison burger eaters wants no bun and no onions, and another wants medium-well with no bacon and with aioli on the side.

Think you're doing the cooks a favor asking for them to omit an ingredient you're not allergic to but don't want to take out on your own? Think again.

The next two weeks between Christmas and just after New Year's weren't any better. Although his head wasn't screwed all the way in, Ken was one of the main players in the kitchen and was the only person besides Ernesto who regularly rocked the nighttime sauté station. There was a huge gap without him. Two other cooks quit without notice. Our pizza cook broke her wrist on Christmas Eve and couldn't work for a while. We hired a new guy on Christmas Day, and he worked one shift and never returned.

The kitchen was so short staffed, we had our brand-new front-of-house manager, Kathy, do some on-the-job line training. Kathy was a wild one and soon became everyone's favorite manager. She wasn't afraid to tell racy jokes or make comments that would make even the guys in the kitchen blush.

She was right there next to us, twelve hours a day, cranking out fish taco setups and toasting burger buns. Cooks will always respect a manager or server more when they can put in the hours and understand how a kitchen works. By the end of the holidays, Kathy had become one of us. We forgot she was even hired on as a front-of-house manager, but she returned to that job soon after the craziness was over.

We all respected her as a leader, not just because of her sense of humor. Although I wasn't a leader in that kitchen yet, I did learn a few lessons from her.

"What's your least favorite task to do at closing?" she asked one day while she was training in the kitchen.

"I really hate plastic wrapping everything," I said without skipping a beat. "I always leave it for last. And someone has always messed up the plastic wrap and I have to untangle it!" I felt my pulse race just thinking about it.

"I'll wrap today," she said.

How do you gain respect from others as a leader? Serve and give people what they need. It doesn't mean you have to bend over backwards and kiss everyone's ass just to get respect. Find the little moments like these that show you actually care, then the respect will come.

Kathy and I worked together pretty well, despite her feeling like she had to tiptoe around me at the beginning after finding out I was a *church girl*, just like the guys did when I first started.

"We all thought you'd have no sense of humor and we would have to stop joking around because you go to church," she said, "but clearly, you have proven us wrong."

One day I mentioned something about church in conversation.

"That always catches me off guard," she said.

"What does?" I replied.

"You being religious," she said.

I worked with other women in that kitchen besides Kathy. In the ever-revolving door of restaurant work, there were quite a few female pantry and prep cooks I worked with. One girl, Maria, held it down on the wheel and grill stations on the main line, and that's not even considering the fact she didn't speak any English. Think working in a busy kitchen is hard? Try doing it when the main form of communication is a language you don't know at all. She worked a few short months before having to return to Mexico just after the holidays that year. The only other woman I worked the main line with there besides Maria and manager Kathy was Thu. She could bust out a full prep list in the time it took me to stuff jalapeno poppers, then hop on the line during a Sunday brunch service and kick just as much ass.

In my ski resort job days, I had become accustomed to working fifteen-plus-hour days. Working those, actually a little less, hours solely in a busy restaurant kitchen slammed from open to past close was a different story. As one of the only restaurants in town open on Christmas Day, we were pulling strings of tickets from the printer long enough to decorate the kitchen in festive, white streamers for the holiday. We were out of prime rib by seven. Around my twelve-hour mark, the chef looked at me and said, "You know, I've worked with very few people your age these days who can put in the hours. Usually, they tell me they can be scheduled for a twelve-hour shift but end up useless after eight hours."

Damn right I can! I could keep going. Sixteen, seventeen hours. Twelve is nothing. Give it to me. I can take anything. It felt good to be praised for something I had been doing for years. I felt proud—accomplished, special because I had something others didn't. I could put in the hours, and he didn't even see my full potential.

"Well," I said with a smirk, thinking back to my ski resort days, "this isn't my first rodeo."

"It's good to know I have someone who can walk the talk and actually do the work, even at the end of a long day," he said.

We served over three hundred people between 6 and 9 p.m., all cooked-to-order dinners. That's excluding the hundreds who showed up during the day for lunch.

And I used to think cooking the same Christmas dinner for twelve at my grandma's house was hard.

Being extremely understaffed during one of the busiest times of the year started to take its toll on everyone, and we could all see it in each other. Normally a smiling, joke-cracking, singing kitchen brigade, we all found ourselves slumping into work each day with our heads down, ready for a beating.

This job was simultaneously physically and mentally exhausting like none other I had worked. There are few jobs like this—jobs where you are required to be operating at full capacity during every single second you are there. In fact, it isn't enough to be doing something at all times. You have to have multiple tasks working at the same time. It's not enough to stand there and stir the risotto. In order to stay afloat, you'll have to remember to stir the risotto in between the ten other tasks you complete in that time, all while keeping an ear out for those working tickets on the line, making sure you don't need to jump in on a rush. Often, you don't have a break. You're lucky if you can go to the bathroom as soon as you need to. Everything is urgent—a fire that needs to be put out right away. If we're out of filet, you can't just say "I'll get to that on Tuesday, after the long weekend. It's Friday afternoon and I'm going to kick back until five." Sure, it is *just food*; we're not saving lives here. But it is people's money, expectations, and your ass on the line if you screw up.

After a fourteen-hour shift a little after New Year's, I knew it was coming. Some kind of impending doom. Do you ever stand up too fast and feel kinda … weird? Like you might pass out but not really, like you feel fuzzy? That's how I felt in a constant state. The rush, the crazy fast pace, the cooking—it was no longer fun. I was going on about twenty days without a day off, and of course, every one of those days required giving 110 percent. *I can't do this much longer. Something's going to snap. This isn't noble or worth glorifying or applauding.*

I thought I had at least a few days before some kind of inevitable meltdown, but the next morning, before work, I found myself curled up in a fetal position on my bed, bawling my eyes out. I felt like such a failure, especially since this wasn't the first or only time I had worked these kinds of hours. I thought I was the one who could handle the workload, like Chef had told me on Christmas. Working that many hours was part of my personality at this point.

Somewhere in the middle of that much-needed crying session, I was mindlessly scrolling through social media, as one does when they are burned out to the point of shutdown, and came across a meme of Gordon Ramsay. In the picture, it looked like he was yelling at some poor cook who had lost the lamb sauce or burned the scallops. The caption said:

When I find myself in times of trouble,
Gordon Ramsay comes to me,
Speaking words of wisdom …
Get your shit together!

And while that wasn't enough to pull me out of my slump entirely, I got a laugh out of the timing of finding that meme, and it became the thread I hung on to for the rest of my day. I had no choice but to pull myself together and show up for my team. I was sure they were just as burnt out as I was.

Just three more days, Hanalei. Three more days, and you get one day off. This was the mantra that kept me going as I numbly cranked out tickets and prepped for another busy night, still feeling like I was in a daze. I remember the very last day of that twenty-two-day streak, I felt I was running a marathon and could see the finish line.

So here's where I should put a neat little paragraph about how I gave up working so much and never burned out again, and how I no longer take pride in being able to work so many hours. But because I was (and still am) young and driven, I took that one day off, felt much better, and bounced right back. Sometimes people are stubborn and don't learn things.

CHAPTER 10

Before the Plague

All seasons have an end, and after the first weekend in January was over, we had our little ski town back. There's something about shared misery that brings a team closer. Maybe it's the stories we recount to each other when we're all on the other side of it. Maybe it's the respect we've gained for each other, knowing the other person holds it down just as hard and can put in the work.

Chef had seen me learning a bit of the nighttime sauté station with Ken before the holidays. Now there was a space for me to fill. In January, I started being scheduled as the full-on sauté cook on Ernesto's midweek days off. We were slow during the week, but it was perfect training for me to learn the station.

Here's how you cook one sea bass entree if you're the sauté cook of the night. First, the cook up front by the ticket printer—the *wheel*—calls out the order. He calls out one sea bass, (that's you!) one seafood tagliarini, (also you, but it only takes three minutes so you're going to wait on this one, but don't forget that!), two filet—one med-rare one medium (mostly the grill cook's job, but you need to have the sides ready). You respond, "Heard," so the wheel knows you heard what he said and will start working on it. You don't want to be in the position where you say "heard," then forget to fire it. You have to remember all your calls. You cannot see the ticket rail. You also are remembering all the items you already have working from before that call, and you have to keep listening out for new calls and add those to your list, while not forgetting about past calls.

So, anyway, sea bass.

All sauté station dishes start with making sure you have a hot pan. Pick one of the twelve burners that's not already in use, and coat the bottom in oil. You start by taking a seven-ounce portion, which you butchered earlier, and rolling it around in the aioli, which the prep cook made but you put in its place by your station earlier as part of your mise. Then you go from the aioli to the pistachio breading, which you also made at some point in time before this dinner service. Once it's coated, it goes in the pan, then the whole pan goes in the oven which is set to 450 but fluctuates because it's opened and closed so much. You can't go by timer because each piece of fish is a different thickness, and it would also be inconvenient to have ten timers for the ten different dishes you have working at the same time. One would go off every thirty seconds, so forget going by time.

Now that the sea bass is in the oven, you can put together the risotto. You made the plain risotto earlier that day (it takes more than fifteen minutes, so it's not cooked to order), so all you have to do is add cream, pesto, and a little parmesan. Always remember to grab every pan handle in any kitchen ever with a towel. Trust me, please learn this the easy way. You have to heat up the risotto, but don't let it get too hot or it'll all stick, but also don't stand there and watch it because you have so much other food working, like steak sides and seafood tagliarini.

It's time to flip the sea bass over. Get in there and use the fish spatula—if you use tongs, the fish may break, and we're all about presentation here. If you flip it and it barely changed color, you messed up. If it's already dark brown or black (burnt) and crispy, you also messed up. Now close the oven before it gets too cold in there.

Now heat up another pan. Are you still watching the risotto? This one needs to get real hot for the zucchini ribbon and cherry tomato garnish. You used a mandolin to get the zucchini into long strips before service. When the oil and the pan are hot enough, the vegetables should sizzle—like really sizzle, maybe even make a little flame when they hit the pan. Get used to the flames; it happens all the time.

Toss those a few times with your sauté flip you have perfected, and it's almost time to plate up. Check on that sea bass. We don't want it raw inside, but we don't want it cooked through and dry. We also don't want the crust to be burnt. If it is, restart the whole thing. We don't serve that.

Scoop the risotto in a nice round scoop into the bowl. It's one of those big, fancy bowls with a large rim. Then pour the orange-red pepper beurre blanc sauce around the risotto. Bright green pesto risotto, bright orange sauce. Make it pop. You made the beurre blanc sauce right before service like you do every day. You had carefully stirred the butter into the white wine reduction and heavy cream so it didn't break. Then you put it in a container and under the heat lamp at your station. Broken sauce is a big no-no.

If your fish is ready, take that out of the oven and place it on top of the risotto. Then take your cooked zucchini ribbons and make a cool twisty-ribbony thing with them on top of the fish. Stack it tall! You're finally done. Somewhere between the risotto and the veg, you had also made that seafood tagliarini and steak sides, so take those to the expo window too.

That was how you make one sea bass entree. Now imagine, if you will, having seven of those working at a time, all started at different times, in different phases of cooking. You're not the sea bass cook, you're the sauté cook, so at the same time you were also making every steak side, every pasta dish, every airline chicken dish— anything from a pan or the oven. You have twelve stove burners—use them all! And like we talked about earlier, you can't see the rail or the orders. You have to remember everything called. It's already hot in the kitchen (obviously) but you're reaching in and out of a 450-degree oven the whole time. At the same time, you remembered not to grab any pans without a towel, and you kept track of your tongs the whole time.

Most of us barely make anything above minimum wage, and in certain states, the people who cooked your food are not allowed to get tips.

***

I continued working sauté station through January, but I was still being paid my starting wage (which was the company minimum, based on my small amount of experience), even though I was one of the very few cooks who could now work every single station. It was time for that to change. Actually, it had been time for that to change for a while, but I was waiting around for management to notice. I mean, my actions should be enough, right? Why would I have to use talk to be paid what I'm worth?

I asked Chef. His eyes widened. "You're still getting paid what you did when you started?"

"Yes," I said.

"That needs to change. We'll talk more on Friday," he said.

Yes, your actions should be what gets you a raise, not talk, but sometimes, all you have to do is ask. Pay shouldn't be a taboo topic in the workplace. How do you think people have found discrepancies and inequalities? By keeping it a secret?

During that conversation on Friday, I earned the raise and told Chef I wanted to continue learning and growing. This industry, along with all its hardships, characters, and quirks, had me for the long haul. Just like the ski resort, there was plenty of opportunity for leadership, growth, and stepping out of my comfort zone. At the end of our conversation, on the note of wanting to grow and learn, I said, "If you want to put me on sauté on a Friday or Saturday night, you can go ahead and do so," almost just as a gesture for something that may happen way in the future. I had barely started working the station anyway. I had no idea how I would fare if it were busy.

We walked back to the kitchen, and Chef started talking to Ernesto. Ernesto looked at me with that mysterious, wordless smile, and handed me over his station. Then I realized it *was* Friday.

Fast forward to about seven o'clock—I'm drowning in fish tacos watching the wild, après ski crowd take ski shots (usually four to six shot glasses in a line attached to a ski, all lifted up at the same time—the epitome of ski town night life in the winter). On Fridays we did a fish taco special, and of course that all came from sauté. I felt like every ticket was dragging food from my station, and I was the weak link. Both ovens had decided to stop working, so I was improvising by searing everything in a pan, then walking across the line to the salamander (it's like a broiler up top that we use for melting cheese and toasting) to finish it off. That's what line cooks do—we can't stop serving food because there's a problem. We think on our feet, solve it, then keep on cooking. All that matters is at the end of the night, everyone got their food on time, everything looked good, and nothing was sent back. And that's what happened that night. There's no such thing as a perfectly smooth, busy night, and that's something I've become accustomed to slowly. Chef started putting me on Friday night sauté so I could continue practicing the station while it was busy.

As the winter continued, everything seemed to be going great. I was progressing every day at work, being given more responsibilities. I made it through Presidents' Day week, which in our ski town was just as big as the holidays. Trevor, the kitchen lead, broke his hand and was out for a few months, which gave me an opportunity to take over most of what he did. For the first time at the job, I had a chance to lead again. I would come into work every day and be greeted with a chorus of "Prima!" (Spanish for female cousin).

Everything was on an upward trend, including a strange new virus called COVID-19. At first, the virus was a joke—we were far enough away from truly affected areas for it to seem distant and not our problem. Someone would sneeze, and we would all joke and say in a funny voice, "Hanalei has coronavirus, hahahahaha." Then, in mid-March, during a multifoot snowstorm on my twenty-third birthday, the shutdown hit.

CHAPTER 11

Lockdown

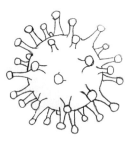

If I knew my twenty-third birthday would be my last time in a restaurant in three months, I would have ordered dessert. In mid-March 2020, the world shut down, including the restaurant where I worked. They said it would only be two weeks.

On the first day of lockdown, I drove through the snow straight to the store and spent two hundred dollars on food, but it wasn't for me. I had a plan. There were limited pickings, and shelves were empty. There was no chicken, beef, or toilet paper. It was a weird time.

I knew I needed something to keep myself occupied. Although unemployment was available, it would take weeks, even months to get any money. Like most people my age living paycheck to paycheck in a ski town, I was going to have to improvise.

Going home with lamb shoulder, shrimp, and Japanese eggplant (the only vegetable left), I started my unofficial business. I had friends and contacts who I knew would be enthusiastic to order food from me. The plan was to cook a family meal every day and have people sign up for delivery. For a while, I had to work around what was available at the store. Sometimes, that meant I had to get creative, using ingredients most families don't cook with. For a while, I couldn't buy chicken, rice, or salt. There was no yeast, flour, or vinegar. I couldn't go with a list. I would buy whatever they had and then go home and plan the family meals, praying people would sign up so I didn't end up with having to finish twelve lamb shanks all on my own, taking the financial loss with it.

My husband and I reached out to everyone we knew locally and told them what we were doing. This was a friends-and-family-only service based on trust and donations. As I seasoned the lamb shoulder and prepared to braise, I built my website where people could order for future dates. I had three families for my first meal, which was a Mediterranean-style lamb shoulder with couscous, pita, and Japanese eggplant. Then God provided customers for the next day and the next. For the first two weeks of lockdown, I had between one and five families of four signed up for my meal deliveries. Easter Sunday was my biggest day of the entire lockdown. I guess being the first holiday since COVID happened, people were eager for a good family meal. I cooked a leg of lamb roast with plenty of sides for forty people. It was the first time in weeks I had cooked for those quantities. And of course, I kept all the profit. For those first few weeks, between the shopping, cooking, planning, delivering and cleanup, it was a full-time job for me.

In addition to cooking and delivering food, I also busted out some of those business skills I had learned in college. I dusted off my accounting notes and tried to keep track of debits and credits, net income, and inventory throughout the whole time. I kept every receipt and meticulously entered every small purchase into my spreadsheet. I built a whole website for people to order their meals from. I marketed it on social media and through word of mouth. I even researched what it would take to get the proper permitting to expand beyond friends and family. I guess my business degree wasn't in vain.

There were a few times when I failed and felt as if I shouldn't be letting my friends and neighbors trust me with their money. Like when I bought a whole pork butt and thought it would feed five families, but when I portioned it out, it turned out to be a lot less, and I had to stretch it and serve less to each family than planned. You can't hide mistakes like that. My order form promised that "meals serve four," but I had a customer reach out to me that day and tell me that the food was great, but it only served two. Or another time when I had people sign up for falafels because I had found a recipe, but I had never actually made falafels before. Winging it has its place, but not when other people's trust and money are at stake. The falafels disintegrated and fell apart if you looked at them too hard, but at that point, it was too late to change anything because it was time to deliver. I did not get a repeat order from those people.

If I learned one thing from this time, it was not to send out something that is subpar and not your best, especially if you know it. Even now, back in the professional kitchen, if I burn something, I remake it and tell them it's going to be a few more minutes. If something's too salty, I don't just "hope they won't notice." People notice. You can't just hide your mistakes. You can try, but don't expect their business again.

Of course, there was positive feedback too. Most of my customers were moms who now had to juggle working from home and distance learning with their kids, who were now at home. They were, understandably, overwhelmed. The last thing anyone wanted to do at that point was navigate the bare shelves of the grocery store, try to improvise meals from what was there, cook, and clean up. I could see the joy and relief in their eyes as I delivered their meals, and it made the entire day's worth of planning, waiting in the mile-long line at the store, and doing dishes worth it all. People told me my meals were "a delight" and "something different." I received one "Best meal I've ever had!" To me, that was worth more than the money. I felt like I did when I heard my first compliment on that medium-rare filet steak when I first started working grill at the restaurant. It wasn't an ego boost. I desperately needed confirmation that cooking was my calling.

I learned that a key to a successful business is to have repeat customers. Most of my business came from the same few families ordering over and over. I had to switch up meals and keep them satisfied. It's one thing to pump up your product on social media and market it to as many people as you can to get a ton of orders. But that will ultimately fail if the product isn't good for the price you're offering. I also learned about keeping customers happy with custom meals. I already mentioned how, as a restaurant cook, I hated modifications. I wish I could have just posted my meal of the day every day and tell people, *tough luck, it is what it is.* But as people found out about my services, they started to reach out to me about custom orders. Many had anniversaries and birthdays during the lockdown and just wanted a nice meal. I wanted to make sure I gave them exactly what they wanted.

During the three-month lockdown, I learned so much about cooking, I actually returned to my job a stronger cook. I learned the five mother sauces from YouTube, proper braising techniques, baking, and breadmaking. I adopted a sourdough starter named Ferris, who I still have and use to this day. I even *tried* to make puff pastry from scratch. (Key word: tried).

Doing my own thing from home was a good way to pass the time, but I missed the restaurant kitchen. It was hard having to find my own customers, compared to working at the always-slammed, swanky downtown restaurant people were literally lining up to get into. Cooking at home had its own challenges, but it didn't give the rush of a busy service or the camaraderie among peers. I missed being around people all day. My heart longed for more interaction than just a quick, contact-free delivery at a doorstep. Didn't we all?

At the end of May, I finally received the call. I would return to work that same day.

CHAPTER 12

Deja Vu

U pon coming back from lockdown, I was reminded of why I loved the kitchen so much—the people.

Ray had been our prep cook since I started. He was a short Filipino stick figure of a guy who carried the whole establishment on the shoulders of his 130-pound frame. He was a workhorse who would bust out an entire prep list in his shift there, then go on to his night job to complete his eighteen-hour workday.

"So sleepy today …" was his catchphrase … every single day. Even still, he would often be caught singing and dancing while prepping. Everyone loved Ray.

"He's trying to save up and become the king of the Philippines," we would joke.

While he prepped in the back, the line cooks would yell out things they needed, and Ray would get it for them without fail. We had a running joke that if anything went slightly wrong, it was his fault. We all agreed the place would fall apart if we didn't have him.

Arjun started just after we reopened. He had moved to the United States from India only four years ago and quickly became the loveable goofball of the kitchen (although every single cook was a goofball in their own way). He started in the pantry but quickly made his way to the wheel station on the main line. Arjun was the first one to come up with the "cleared the rail" dance. It was not unusual, with him on the line, to break out into dance when we took the last ticket off after a rush. We knew he was a good find when, in the middle of a 350-cover Saturday night, the whole line was dancing and singing while busting out tickets on time with no send-backs.

Front of house and back of house worked harmoniously at the restaurant, which I learned was not always the case. That's how it should be anyway, right? It's not front of house versus back of house. It's us versus the dinner rush. There were just as many fun, interesting people out serving tables as there were in the kitchen. Grant was everyone's favorite server, despite making the most mistakes. He was so lovable, he could go up to the kitchen at 8 p.m. on a Saturday, ask for a medium New York strip and a filet on the fly (meaning like, right now) because he forgot to ring it in, and no one would yell at him. He regularly burst out into song, and Grant and I often sang Queen songs at full blast if we were having a good night.

He actually had a pretty good voice and would invent lyrics on the fly, coming up with a song about our jalapeno poppers, our dishwasher, and our male expeditor's voluptuous booty (according to Grant).

"Hello Martine, are the dishes clean? Don't get COVID nineteeeeeeeeen!" he sang to our dishwasher.

"*Pinche gringo*," the dishwasher would say, muttering more Spanish under his breath and shaking his head.

His signature snack was a slider bun, filled with mashed potatoes and dunked in water. One day he lost his server booklet, and the whole restaurant searched for forty-five minutes before he suddenly remembered he had left it in the freezer.

Kevin was Grant's roommate and also our main pizza guy. He was the skier's skier. A classic ski-town local, he could do double backflips and pretzel 270s with ease. He suffered many injuries through skiing, including a broken back that winter before the shutdown. To him, it was worth the send. He was a chill dude with a positive mindset and took it all in his stride. When he was in the "pizza zone," he looked like someone had taken a video of him and sped it up, stretching dough and laying out toppings in smooth, fluid motions with no mistakes. Whoever thinks "slinging pies" is a low-skill job that anyone can do needs to watch this guy on a Saturday night in the pizza zone.

Kevin had a running challenge with Lance, one of the other pizza cooks, to see who could gain the most weight. It didn't matter how, or where on the body, or in what form the weight was gained.

"Women want a man who is strong and can protect them," said Lance.

"Yeah, isn't that right, Hanalei?" said Kevin, turning to the only woman in the kitchen.

"I mean, not really, but maybe for some?" I said, laughing, "I mean, I can't speak for *all* women."

"What do you mean?" said Kevin. "Your husband is ripped!"

"Yeahhhh, riiiiippped!" said Lance, flexing his arms.

They had a point.

Sometimes I'd catch Kevin smashing a triple PB&J, claiming it was his seventh one in a row, or Lance ordering a full prime rib dinner after work, polishing off all sixteen ounces of it. Their Gainz challenge continues the day I write this.

Although we were at limited capacity and all had to wear masks, we added more outdoor seating and were able to get pretty busy. We were running on a much tighter staff than the year before after losing all of our seasonal workforce from South America and Romania due to travel bans and the virus. We cut our staff from five line cooks and two pantry on a busy service to only three line cooks and one pantry, doing the same numbers, if not more. Everyone had to be more efficient, work harder, and be held to higher standards.

It was soon after we reopened from lockdown that the chef started giving me more responsibilities and hinting at another raise. He asked me to start taking on a more supervisory role, even while still scheduled as a full-on line cook. I found myself facing the same challenges as I did at the ski resort. I was one of only a few women, and now I had to take charge over men who were, more often than not, older than me. With a little more confidence than I had then, but still with my insecurities and doubt, I picked up where I had left off.

One of the hardest parts for me was gaining respect. This isn't just an issue for women leading in male-dominated fields. This is an issue for any leader, especially in the workplace, because people don't always want to be there, and they don't get to choose their boss. Have you ever worked with a boss who may have a title but clearly doesn't have the respect from their peers? A company can make an announcement about a new leader, hold a meeting to tell everyone to report to them, maybe even have consequences for not listening to that leader, but at the end of the day, you can't force genuine respect. There were several lessons about gaining respect I had to learn as I began the journey of learning to lead. In fact, many of these are an ongoing process, which I expect to continue well after writing this book.

In an environment such as a kitchen, where everyone is expected to work hard as a team, gaining respect isn't enough. Maintaining it daily is the real battle. Every single day I walk into the kitchen is a fight to keep respect, and I'm grateful for every person who kept me in check. Without the people who questioned my authority, pushed back, and checked my work, I wouldn't have learned what I did so early on in my journey. One of these people was Juan.

Juan was a quiet Hispanic man in his fifties who had years, maybe even decades of line cooking experience before we hired him on at the beginning of that summer. This guy knew what it took to work in a kitchen and could smell BS from a mile away. He would often call it out without saying a word. If I, or anyone else prone to talking too much, became caught up yapping away while prepping in the back while Juan was stuck with tickets on the line, he would make the "talking" hand gesture, often followed with a "mucho blah blah blah."

Juan would often set up the entire line on his own in the morning, filling up every station before the restaurant opened. By the time I would arrive for my swing shift around noon, he had already put in hours of hard work, and he expected the same from everyone else. Of course, I was also there to work just as hard, but as a leader, I was often spread between helping Juan on the line, dinner prep, pantry, putting away deliveries, and answering questions from everyone. Often I found myself spread thin, not being able to give him my full attention on the line. To Juan, this sometimes looked like laziness. I could tell he thought this of me, when I knew that I was not lazy, and I honestly didn't know how to deal with it. To add to it, I didn't speak much Spanish at the time, and he didn't speak great English, so while we communicated enough to work together, we couldn't just sit down and talk it out.

I was beginning to get frustrated with him, but I also saw how much hard work he was doing, and I did value him as an employee. I wanted to show him I was working hard but also didn't want to make it seem like I was just kissing his ass so he wouldn't be mad at me, which made me even more frustrated because I was his superior at work after all, and I felt it was becoming the other way around. I told Chef about my struggles with Juan, not as a telling-on-him way, but more just to voice some of my struggles as a new leader.

"I left the line to do orders, since there were no tickets, and I hear Juan say, 'where did she go? *El baño?*' and I tried to explain to him I was doing orders, but he wasn't having it!" I said. Chef had just started training me to place produce orders at the time, and I would try to do them after I had covered all my other bases. Doing the job at hand came before my own growth. I continued, "It's hard because he thinks I'm lazy when I work just as hard as he does. Imagine if someone were to actually be lazy around him. He would have none of it!"

"Trust me, I face the same thing and I'm the chef of this place," he said. "I also have to earn that respect every single day from people like Juan. The key is being able to communicate to him what you have to do besides just help him on the line, while also showing him you have his back."

Even with the title, the experience, and being a man, he still had to earn that respect. Maintaining respect will always be something a leader has to stay aware of.

One day, I felt I was doing well switching among all my responsibilities—prepping, answering questions, and delegating, when we were hit with a sudden rush of tickets. I jumped right on the line with Juan and started slinging fish tacos and working the fryer, listening to him call out tickets and helping him plate up where needed.

At the end of the rush, I returned to my prep task. He held out his hand for a fist bump. "You *numero uno*," he said.

And although that seems like a nice, bow-tied wrap-up to a story about gaining Juan's respect, it's not. Maintaining respect is the hard part. There were days after that I could feel him keeping me in check. Every day is a balance, and sometimes you do feel like you're people pleasing. What matters is that people feel you have their back, and the respect will follow.

Soon after all this, I also downloaded a language-learning app and started learning Spanish.

***

Some people let authority go to their head. I seemed to have the opposite problem. Soon, I was in charge of making sure we were all ready for dinner service, including pantry and pizza station. I hated being the person "walking around with a clipboard," but sometimes it was what I had to do. In my mind, the clipboard symbolized the overpaid, lazy manager at a construction site wearing a business suit and a fresh, clean hard hat who didn't do any actual work, which is far from what I was as a leader. Just like my very first shot at leadership at the ski resort, I was not used to having any authority, and I had a hard time separating laziness from delegating.

There was this moral dilemma in my head about asking people to do things that I could do myself. There was nothing unethical about asking someone else to peel potatoes if I knew I didn't have time because I had to butcher steak. For some reason, asking people to peel potatoes specifically made me feel like a terrible person. *Would Jesus peel his own potatoes? Would he make John or Bartholomew do it for him?* I told Chef almost jokingly about my moral dilemma of potatoes.

"It would be different if you asked them to peel your potatoes then walked around with a clipboard for half an hour," he said, "but they see you're still working while they peel. That's why they will still respect you. They know you won't have time for the potatoes because you're breaking down tenderloins, and that's a skill they don't have."

It was deja vu. I felt like I was living through that same experience I had right after being promoted at the ski resort. There I was—a fresh leader, learning on the fly, as a young woman in a male-dominated workplace. I was building upon all the lessons I had learned there, in just as short of a time period, winging it on the daily.

My perspective was shifting from just being able to cook, to being responsible for other people's cooking. Someone else's mistake was no longer "not my problem." If the pizza guy was caught standing around on the clock, it was my fault for not seeing it. If the guy making the ahi poke was putting too much poke on the plate, it was my responsibility. As a leader, there is no more saying, "Well, it wasn't *me*," and no more making up excuses for your own mistakes. Many times, I caught myself making excuses and eventually had to own up to my mistakes and fix the issue. Before, as an entry-level employee, I could take pride in the fact that "I'm the only one who can do such-and-such right, or "no one can do this specific task as well as I do." As a leader, me being the only one who can do a task right is an issue. It now meant I wasn't calling out other people's mistakes or correcting problems when I saw them. It was a difficult mindset shift for me. It used to be "not my mistake, not my problem. I'm just here to cook," and was now "I'm here to make this restaurant run better and to avoid wasted product or labor." Holding down a grill full of steaks was now the easiest, most base-level skill of my job. *I miss the days when the dinner rush was the hardest part of my job.*

RECIPE

Ray's Special Sweet and Sour Sauce

1 cup apple cider vinegar
1 cup white vinegar
1/2 cup sugar
1 jalapeño pepper
1 teaspoon chili flakes
1 red onion

Finely slice the red onion and jalapeño.
Mix all ingredients together.
Sauce will keep for months in the fridge. It is ready to use as a marinade or over your favorite meats.

Goes great on carne asada-type beef, like skirt steak or off-cuts. We would always use it on prime rib scraps we would end up with after slicing the rest up for cheesesteak. It can give cooked chicken or pork that extra zing. How excited we all were when Ray busted out the sauce and we knew it was snack time.

CHAPTER 13

Growing Pains

The learning never seemed to stop, and I was embracing it all with open arms. That's what I always looked for in a job, and I was happy I had found a place that was giving it to me. Some lessons were harder to learn than others. We all have skills we may be naturally good at. I'm sure you're also aware there are things that do not come naturally for you. For me, one of those skills was organizing. Unless it was my mise for my station, I could not organize a walk-in or dry storage to save my life. My home kitchen was the same way. It wasn't messy or dirty (in fact, it might even pass a health inspection), but nothing had a place. I would unload the groceries at home and throw them at random onto shelves until I could shove the cupboard door shut.

Apparently, women are supposed to be naturally good at this. As a wife, I'm supposed to be the one telling her husband that he "put the dishes away wrong," so much that he gives up and the wife is condemned to doing the dishes until death does them part. I had sworn I would not be "that woman."

"What do you see wrong with this?" Chef would say, taking me aside to look at one of the walk-ins.

With all my might, I would try to look around at the shelves and figure out what he was trying to show me. I wanted to prove I wasn't totally clueless. I was anything but lazy, but I truly thought the walk-in looked fine.

"Looks fine to me," I would finally say.

He then spent the next hour having me throw away empty boxes, put root vegetables with other root vegetables, and condense sauces. I just had to be taught what to see.

"Chef is really hounding you about this, isn't he?" said Lance. Even other people noticed how hard Chef had to work just to have me notice small things out of place.

I don't think Chef knew how bad I was at this until he started training me on it. All these hours he's spent teaching me to organize, and I was still far below average. How could someone possibly be so bad at something?

Once I was shown exactly how everything should be, I started to get the hang of it and was able to be a more effective leader because of it. Soon, I could even train new guys on keeping the walk-ins, dry storage, and shelves organized.

Could I now walk into a different kitchen and organize it without anyone showing me? No. Can I keep the kitchen I work in and am shown where everything should be organized? Yes. Sometimes, I catch myself now saying, "Hey, which one of you guys put the dishes away wrong?"

Now I am "that woman." At least at work I am.

***

Even after a year of working the line at that place, I was still finding ways to be a better line cook. I was learning the importance of having a strong lead on the wheel station and found it harder to be the one calling tickets and organizing orders than just cooking food to order. I learned to keep a clean work surface, and always put everything back in the exact place it belonged. I learned the key to keeping a busy service flowing was to be in constant communication with the expo and every cook in the kitchen. I learned terms like, "Next pickup!" which means the next few items you need to complete a table, and I practiced always responding with a "heard" or always waiting to get a "heard" back after calling something out. It was like using the radios at the mountain ops job. You couldn't just yell something out into the void. You had to address someone specifically by name, get a response from them, then say what you need to say. You have to be assertive in leading the line. It's, "I need that BBQ chicken right now!" Not, "Please, good sir on sauté, if you would do so, this is a gentle reminder that you have a BBQ chicken on order. But please, no pressure, it will be ready when you are ready."

A silent line is a disorganized line. I learned to jump on and take the reins in the middle of a Sunday brunch service, when the line was in disarray, lacking any communication. I would step in and figure out what our first three pickups were, make sure everything was working, and within ten minutes the line would be organized and caught up.

I would delegate prep tasks between all the different cooks, and people were reporting directly to me. I told people when they could go home. When I first was given the authority to send people home or keep them, I was so focused on cutting labor that I would get as many people off the clock as possible, only to find myself scrambling during dinner service because I didn't have enough prep. This was a learning experience that resulted in many failed services and frantic nights cutting vegetables to order. Sometimes, people's forty-dollar entrees suffered because of it.

As a twenty-three-year-old and one of two women in a large kitchen, I'm not going to pretend like there weren't times I felt as if my authority was diminished because of it. A few times, I would tell someone to do something, only to find them a minute later asking Trevor about what they should do, as Trevor was the other leader in the kitchen. We were equal in authority under the chef at this time. I think some of them had never seen a woman in authority in their workplace and didn't know how to react. For some of them, it could have just been their individual upbringing and culture. I didn't take offense; if anything, I was happy to be the first.

One time, Arjun said to me as I was closing down the entire line by myself and finishing up mopping the floor, "You are girl! Why do they make you work this hard?"

"What does that have to do with anything?" I said. "This is my job. I'm held to the same standards as you guys."

I didn't want to see age or gender as a roadblock or an excuse not to work to be the best leader and cook I could be. Instead of focusing on the aspects I couldn't control, I focused on what I could. For example, being competent at the job at hand. Age, gender, social status, or any factor like that won't matter if you can't work every station, prep any item on the prep list, or aren't willing to get down and dirty cleaning the bottom of the dish pit after a Friday night service.

I also found that discovering my own leadership style rather than trying to conform myself to what society thinks a kitchen leader should look like helped me gain the confidence I needed. Maybe I didn't have to bark orders like those chefs on TV. I once heard being a leader referred to as a "masculine" trait. I would disagree. Leadership looks different on everyone. It's better if we can work with our strengths and integrate them into our style rather than change who we are at the core. Maybe a woman in leadership doesn't need to make herself more masculine to gain respect and hold authority in a male-dominated environment. Maybe such an environment can actually benefit from having feminine traits in leadership. If we are comfortable being who we are in our role, then we can be more confident. People notice when a leader has confidence.

***

I liked having to train the new guy because they were like a blank slate. I trained a few of them during that summer. I once heard a saying, "What's more expensive than training someone then having them quit? Not training them and having them stay."

A new guy was an opportunity to train all the right habits from day one. It also made me look at my own habits and if I was taking shortcuts. What authority would I have if I told them to do it one way, then cut a corner myself? It's so much easier to set the standard from day one and live it out yourself in front of new hires, rather than have to untrain bad habits.

Just like the guys had trained me on the grill when I first started, I came full circle and trained others on my beloved grill station. I realized I couldn't just be the Grill Queen if I wanted to progress. A true leader will pass on his or her skills to the next up-and-coming person. If I hogged my favorite station and didn't let anyone else work it, I would be failing as a kitchen leader. If I knew that steaks and burgers wouldn't come off the grill perfect if I wasn't there, I had failed. A bad leader is someone who thinks, *This place would fall apart if I weren't here 24/7.* A good leader knows if they aren't there for a bit, it will be fine because they've trained up good hands for the place to be in.

I taught them all the small details to make sure the steaks were leaving the kitchen nothing less than perfect, even if I was not the one grilling. I taught them to pick the right shape steak for each temperature, how to flip the steak for perfect grill marks every time, and I had them start off using a thermometer, just like I did. Arjun was one of the first people I fully trained on the grill. I'd start letting him cook one or two under my watch on a slow night. Then I would be more hands-off and just check it before it hit the plate. One night, while I was on sauté and he was on grill/wheel, we had one of those huge tables that all ordered steak at all different temperatures. Those were my favorite tables.

"You got this, or do you want me to handle this table?" I asked.

"No, I got this," he said.

I let him have at it. I checked the five rib-eyes and five filets before they left. I didn't need to. They were all perfect.

***

None of this learning came without some hardship. Having more responsibility and at times, what felt like so little control was beginning to wear on me. Everything seemed to be happening so fast. A year ago, I had been the quiet, shy new girl who couldn't believe the biggest restaurant in town had given her a chance on the line. I had so little experience and no formal cooking education, and suddenly I found myself being given all these opportunities. Every day felt like I was flying by the seat of my pants, trying to figure out how to build a raft in the middle of a storm at sea. For the most part, I welcomed it all.

In mid-July, there was a series of events, all within a week, that made me seriously consider switching jobs. First, after a Sunday brunch service, Chef called me into his office. I didn't know if it would be good or bad. He proceeded to show me an email from the general manager about my performance the previous Saturday night after the chef had left. I was in charge of training our newest hire, Carl, and after the main dinner rush was over, Chef and Ernesto left, which was okay on their part, given it was almost close and we didn't need so many cooks. We didn't think we would get much business after that, but we did get one more small push—nothing more than two cooks should have been able to handle. Carl burned his finger and couldn't get over it and became essentially useless for the rest of the night, which left me working all five stations by myself. The GM had said in the email that I was, "A deer in headlights when it gets busy." He also wrote that Carl was sneaking free food, sometimes cooking himself an extra chicken wing, and that he was not following basic hygiene practices. This was all happening right under my watch. Remember how, as a supervisor, everything that wasn't my problem is now my problem? Carl's constant munchies were my fault.

"I'm giving you all the tools and opportunities you need to succeed, and you're not using them," said Chef, frustrated at the email after spending almost two months training me up as the next supervisor. *How had I not said anything to Carl? I saw him and didn't say anything. Why was I such a pushover again? Why did I suck at my job?* All these thoughts started to consume me for the following week, and it only became worse.

There were a few company policies that honestly, I had become a little lax in upholding. Now that I was a lead in the kitchen, it was my job to enforce rules. For example, if a mistake order is made, we throw it away and write it down on the waste sheet. No ifs, ands, or buts. If we want a shift meal, we ring it in. That same week I had the meeting with Chef, I was caught letting the dishwasher guy eat one of our honest mistakes, and I was called out for it. I felt like a failure. *I'm not cut out for this. How can I lead others if I'm not even following policies myself? I'm too much of a softie. I can handle the heat of a rush, but not the heat of being a leader.*

All the good I had done seemed to go out the window. I felt as if nothing I did right was being noticed by managers, and everything wrong had a magnifying glass on it. It was deja vu, only I knew exactly when I had felt this before. Just like that day, sitting on the chairlift ranting to Matt about all the ways I was leading and delegating right going unnoticed, I was facing the same battles. Every day I would walk into the kitchen, check in with prep, line, and pantry, create a full list, and either do or delegate every task. I always stepped up to cover for someone else no-showing (a common occurrence), showed up early, and stayed late. Dinner services were successful for the most part, and whenever I was unprepared, I still was able to pull through and make it happen. But I guess none of that mattered. I was still being paid the same as the pizza guy and was doing all this work in hopes of a raise that kept getting dangled in front of me. I started to look for other jobs.

CHAPTER 14

Kicking Ass and Cooking Sea Bass

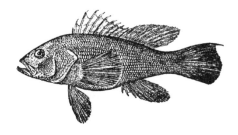

There were many times that summer where I woke up in a sweat from yet another work dream. These dreams mostly took two forms. In one, I had a grill full of steaks all going on medium well and I couldn't move to take them off (because, well, I was lying in bed). In the other, our expo (the one whose voluptuous booty had its own song from Grant) was asking me for tickets, "I need table 7's entrees now!" or "I need fries to sell!" and half my brain knew I was in bed on my day off, while the other half was panicking because I couldn't move to get the food in the window.

Starting the week I felt my job was going south, we started to get slammed every single day. We had just finished putting up a huge outdoor seating structure and could now seat even more people than we could pre-COVID. The weather was nice, and the tourists were here. I was still working grill/wheel most nights, and I covered Ernesto for sauté on Tuesdays and Wednesdays. We were still running bare-bones staff during the week, and I was getting my ass handed to me every single day, especially those Tuesdays and Wednesdays. I was the B-team sauté cook. Sure, I had worked a Friday/Saturday here and there in February, but summer was our big season. Every sauté day, I struggled to get my mise en place before 5 p.m., and I had to do it all by myself because there was only one other cook on duty, who would be caught up with watching tickets on the line nonstop. I would lie to myself and say I'd finish my prep between tickets because "it's Wednesday, and it will be slow." We would then work through a 250-cover night with only two line cooks and one pantry cook.

For a few months, I did nothing but work and sleep. On my one day off, I would wake up at noon, still groggy and burned out from the week, and I would usually spend the day doing absolutely nothing. I didn't even want to cook a nice meal for myself, which was usually how I wanted to spend my day off. This is the cook's dilemma: we're in it because we love food, but we spend so much time cooking for others, we can't be bothered to cook our own. I never cooked my own meals on the days I worked, but on my day off, you better believe I'm going all out or not cooking at all. It's a huge tomahawk steak with blue cheese compound butter and garlic fingerling potatoes or its frozen pizza. It's large sea scallops with beurre blanc sauce or ice cream and chips for dinner. There's no in-between.

As I thought about moving to another restaurant to get paid what I was worth, I couldn't help but think of what I would leave behind. I applied to one, but when they responded to me to set up an interview, I paused. I didn't know what the work culture would be like there. Would it be as fun and harmonious? Would I have to start way at the bottom again, and would there be any opportunity for me to progress? Will there be a Grant to sing Queen songs with? A Trevor to overthrow the government with? What about Ray or Kathy or Ernesto? Will there be someone like Ken to constantly teach and mentor me (in cooking, not scam prevention)? Will there be an Arjun dancing when we clear the rail, or a Kevin to get stoked about ski season with? I did not respond to the other restaurant.

When I realized that God had me at that specific restaurant at that specific time, things started to turn for the better. I stepped up in my leadership role and continued delegating prep, looking out for the good of the company, and leading the line through rushes. I started to take every company policy seriously. After showing Chef through my actions that I was serious about looking out for the restaurant as a leader and not just myself, I earned that raise. In that conversation, I asked if we ever did titles in the kitchen.

"Is there ever a sous chef here," I asked, "or a kitchen manager?"

"We don't do titles in this company besides head chef," he said, "but I would consider you my sous chef. I never had a title at my last place where I was basically the sous. It's about the authority you've earned through trust, and how you hold yourself as a leader. A title means nothing if you don't have the respect through being a good leader."

"What do I tell people when they ask if I'm the sous chef here?" I said, since people had been wondering. I would always say *"basically"* or *"We don't really do titles here."*

"Ask them, 'what do you think?' A title won't matter if no one sees you as a leader," he said.

***

In between the dinner rushes, somehow there was still time for good conversations. One day, Kevin came up to me and essentially invited himself to my church. I happily told him the time and location and told him to come on by. He said he had been searching for *something* his whole life and had tried going to a local church at one point.

"They make you sit and stand at different times, and I was just so confused by all the rituals," he said. "Then there was this part where the priest goes around with that dangling smoke thing, and you have to chant some phrase, and he got mad at me because I didn't know it."

"Oh, our church isn't like that," I said, bringing up flashbacks in my mind to my grandma's (the Burmese one) church we were forced to go to when we visited her as kids. "There aren't rituals or rules, and we don't really have a denomination. We just follow Jesus."

That summer, he actually did show up at church one Sunday. The next week, he was baptized with us in the river. I was able to watch before rushing off to work a Sunday brunch service.

Then there was a server who found out that his roommate knew me and attended my church. When we talked about church, he mentioned how someone told him he was going to hell because he had to work on Saturdays, the Lord's day. Yet there we were, at work, on a Saturday. Jesus was the biggest rule-breaker of his time. He broke Sabbath rules by healing people on the holy day and chastised the Pharisees and religious leaders of the time for being so stuck in their ways. He committed the huge no-no of talking to a woman who wasn't in the racial group he was supposed to talk to. He literally overturned the tables of religion when he saw the injustices happening in the temple.

I also had many of those conversations with Trevor, whose upbringing had put him off church all together. One day he came up to me and said, "You know, I think I'm starting to realize that maybe there is a God. God is love. I'm still not open to any sort of religion, but I'm open to there being a God."

***

At the beginning of August, still in peak tourist season, Ernesto told the chef he would need a few weeks off to take care of his mom, who had a big surgery. He couldn't say no. Our main sauté cook would be gone during what are historically the two busiest weeks of the whole year, the time around Labor Day weekend. In a tourist town near a lake, in the main restaurant on the main downtown strip, Labor Day weekend was kind of a big deal. In addition, the COVID numbers were supposedly going down, and we were allowed to seat people indoors while keeping the huge outdoor structure. We had more seating at the restaurant than we had ever had before. Somehow, I was the one who was going to take over the station while he was gone. *How did I, the B-team, Tuesday night, only-been-there-a-year, only woman on the main line sauté cook become next in line to cover a seasoned veteran like Ernesto for the busiest time of the year? Can I actually do this? Or is this when they finally find out I'm a fraud?*

So, there I found myself, at eight thirty on a Friday night, fresh out of two of the key parts of our most popular entrees, while also keeping a running and ever-growing list in my head of prep I was running dangerously low on (creamy horseradish, minced garlic, will to carry on, etc.) I watched Chef pick up my slack and make mashed potatoes from scratch, to order, and hack away at a frozen block of sea bass because I had failed to even thaw, let alone butcher enough for service. I was frantically slicing zucchini at the deadly mandolin while working a full rail of tickets, still amazed today at how I didn't end up taking half my finger off.

And yes, I had been cooking professionally for a few years, and yes, I'd worked through busier nights than that, but I realized I was still not beyond wanting nothing more than to retreat into the walk-in and put a bucket over my head, just like those first few months at the seafood spot. Some people have this crazy idea that I'm good at cooking because I do it for a living—that I've mastered my job and craft. I used to have this crazy idea that if I worked in a restaurant kitchen long enough, I'd eventually stop getting my ass kicked. At the end of that night, beaten down and trying not to think about how it wasn't even Labor Day weekend yet and how it would only get busier, I promised myself I would be more prepared the next day. I pulled myself together, because that's what you do when you have to perform at 100 percent every day, even if your 100 percent doesn't cut it.

The next day, I walked into work like any other Saturday, greeting all my *primos* with enthusiasm, smiling, cracking jokes. I started boiling potatoes (precisely twice as much as Friday), helped the day crew on the line for a little, started my beurre blanc sauce, made risotto, and made sure we had enough sea bass butchered. Dinner prep was going very smoothly. The day started so optimistic.

Then Chef pulled Trevor aside because Trevor seemed to be angry at him about something. The whole kitchen peered through the one-foot-by-one-foot window, watching them argue outside—two alpha-male lions in one of those nature documentaries, about to fight. You couldn't hear it, but you could feel it.

My attention was quickly drawn away when I noticed the flames. The entire stove range was on fire. Ray and a few others had noticed it too, and we began dumping salt, but it wasn't going out. As I continued to pour salt, I noticed the flames were actually behind the stove, and then it clicked.

The propane lines are all back there. It's not just the stove on fire anymore. This whole thing could blow! And I'm only a foot away from it!

Meanwhile, the unrelenting Saturday lunch continued in full force. Tickets lined the rail as two cooks continued to power through, grilling burgers and battering fish and chips like it was just another summer day. *Don't mind me here. We're all good. Everything's fine.*

"Here, I have water!" said Arjun, picking up a bucket of water, ready to dump it on the grease fire.

Several people damn-near wrestled him away from that situation.

By now, a few managers and servers had realized it was more than just a little flame and joined in pouring salt. The flames began to die down, and soon we had it under control.

Then Trevor and Chef came in from outside.

"What did we miss?" said Chef, looking around at piles of salt and lingering flames, as the dust settled. We all stared in silence as our once-harmonious kitchen now resembled the disaster trail of a tornado. I looked at the time. It was four thirty. Dinner orders would start coming in by five—rain, shine, or huge kitchen fire. Never mind the fact that I thought I was going to die ten minutes ago. All I could think about now was how behind I was on prep.

"What do you need?" asked Chef. I came up with a list. The hardest part about nighttime sauté is not necessarily the dinner service itself but all the small, more sophisticated prep items that go into it, and having to meet that hard deadline of 5 p.m. every single day. This wasn't a time to be a strong, independent woman who don't need no one to help her. This wasn't *my* station and *my* prep. This was our kitchen. This was our Saturday dinner service. There were plenty of times I had helped Kevin and Lance with pizza or Ray with prep. The past few days covering sauté had helped me realize that it was more than okay; actually it was encouraged to have my turn.

When the clock struck five, we were ready. The mess was cleaned up, the potatoes were mashed, the basil was chiffonaded, and our heads were in the right place.

Do you ever have those days when you feel like you're in exactly the right place at the right time? Like a calling-affirming moment? That Saturday night was one of those. My hope for everyone is to find their thing, whether it's a career, a passion, or some other calling. What makes your eyes light up when you talk about it? What makes you want to push through difficult moments because you know you'll come out stronger? Whatever that calling is for you, I hope you have those days that make you think, *yes, this is what I'm meant to do.* You might have days when you question it, that's a given. But never forget those days that are 100 percent confirmation that you're on the right track.

Our small team pulled through, sent out 350 covers flawlessly, on time, with no send-backs, complaints, or frantic on-the-fly moments. We didn't even eighty-six anything. AKA, I handed the ass back. Thus is the cycle of working a job that challenges and stretches you daily, leaving you winded even after your hundredth time doing it. You get your ass kicked on Friday, then you kick ass on Saturday, but right when you think you're past getting beat up, you get it kicked again. Such is the circle of ass-kicking.

"Way to bounce back from a rough start," said Chef.

Rough start? Oh yeah, the huge fire. Forgot about that.

That was just a warmup for the big weekend. Every single day since Ernesto left, I had struggled to have all my mise for dinner ready by 5 p.m. sharp. I wondered how I, the young woman with so many doubts, so many shortcomings, and so much more to learn, had become a leader and main sauté cook at the busiest restaurant in town. Every day that week was busy, but it ramped up more and more until its peak on Saturday and Sunday. Which side of the circle of ass-kicking was I going to be on this time?

So there I found myself, squeeze-bottling lines of red pepper sauce over a seafood taglairini dish on the 400-cover Sunday night of Labor Day weekend, thinking to myself, *Out of all the places I could be on a holiday weekend night, why here? What's dragging? Ugh, it's all from my station! Am I going to make it through this? Don't think about that burn on your arm. Shit, I got sea bass burning. What's my next pickup? Ahhhhhhhhhhhh!*

But I pushed on, and before we knew it, only a few tickets remained, and we were still standing. I felt just like I did after my first time in the weeds—beaten down yet triumphant at the same time—only this time, I felt like I had won the battle overall.

We kept cooking until an hour after close; then it was time to clean. Yes, the cooks have to clean up after our long shift, putting out all those plates. We aren't too good to mop the floor, and we aren't above scrubbing down all the stainless steel. Some places have kitchen porters, whose sole job is to clean up after the cooks. Many restaurants, however, do not have them. In a way, I think it's good to have to clean up after yourself. It's a constant reminder for me that I'm never "too good," and it helps me as a leader because I like to say that I wouldn't ask people to do something I wouldn't do. Nothing keeps an ego in check like having to empty the grease trap from the dishwasher when it backs up.

That entire night, the only feedback I received on the food was that one seafood pasta dish was overcooked. They didn't send it back, but they just thought they'd let the chef know. *Oof, I don't even get a second chance to remake it for them. That's the worst.* Of course, I was disappointed in myself after hearing this. I have a high standard for the food I put out, and I also can't stand overcooked seafood. I wished I could have gone out there and explained to the customer that yes, I am capable of cooking right, but somewhere in the frenzy, I screwed up their expensive meal. I can think about the one, or about the other 399. I'm not excusing it or saying it's okay to serve subpar food, but I am saying it's easy to get hung up on one comment. This is all I have to base my entire night's performance off. As a cook, the only feedback you receive is often negative, unless someone is kind enough to specifically say they liked their meal and the server isn't too busy to remember to tell the kitchen. Maybe the other 399 people just had the best meal of their lives. Who knows? I guess we'll never find out. Through my short time as a restaurant cook, I have learned you have to focus your mind on the right thing, while still addressing and fixing the negative feedback where possible.

In a way, being a leader is like being a restaurant cook. No one says anything unless you screw up. If I know this, I can learn to be more confident in myself as a leader, realizing my own wins and correcting the negative feedback.

At the end of that long shift, my arm still covered in fresh burn bubbles while I scrubbed down all the cutting boards, I thought about my first Labor Day Sunday at the seafood spot. I thought about how far I had come since I had first walked into the seafood spot, with no experience in restaurants or leadership. While cranking out lobster rolls and fried shrimp, we were able to think on our feet, laugh at ourselves, and overcome a crazy rush to still deliver all those meals on time. That was the first time I felt like I was getting the hang of working a line, even if the food was much simpler. Now, exactly two years later, at a restaurant just down the street, I was still getting my ass kicked just as hard, but I was learning to roll with it.

I'm pretty sure that weekend, the whole kitchen deserved a "Nice work, boys!" Oh wait, "Nice work, boys and girls!"

AFTERWORD

This book is only the beginning. I was still twenty-three when I wrote this, and I'm not pretending to have it all figured out. Some have cautioned me against publishing a memoir at this age, saying it would be better to reflect on these events decades later with a different mindset. While I agree that our perspectives will change as we grow older and mature, I think there's a benefit in writing it now rather than waiting. In a way, I was still working through a lot of the learning, and still in the same early-twenties mindset. I hope that people in the same age group and walk of life will be able to relate more to something written by someone still in the thick of it. I knew my story wasn't over, and I struggled with writing the end, since the end of the book was just the beginning of my life and my journey.

There is still so much more for me to learn, not only as a cook, but as a leader. I consider this book a memoir of a life in progress, or a recounting of the beginning of my journey. I learned to have confidence in myself, even if I was the only woman and the youngest. It didn't matter if I was building terrain parks or cooking steak.

My message to women who want to work in a male-dominated field or become a leader in their workplace would be: Get out there and do it! Stay humble and focus on becoming competent at the job at hand. Don't be afraid to start at the bottom, but also know your worth. Be aware of the stereotypes often had about women, and the casual sexism that is rampant in such fields. For example, it was not uncommon for me to hear comments such as these:

If one of the guys had an attitude or was being moody, another guy would tell him,

"Why don't you go change your tampon and come back?"

If some of the guys were taking too long to get ready, another would say, "All right, ladies, let's go!" They'd all be dressed, ready, and out the door in ten seconds.

My response in these situations was often—nothing. I know that sounds weak and may not be the story you were hoping to get from a book about a woman killing it in male-dominated fields. But in those moments, I didn't know what to say. Part of it was that I had only known workplaces where I was the only, or maybe one out of two, women. What was "normal" behavior at work anyway? In all my jobs, I knew that my boss and HR would be on my side in a heartbeat, but I didn't see sexist comments such as these (some arguably worse, but I don't feel like repeating them) as a problem at first, because they weren't directed specifically at me. I knew in my mind that I would report any harassment aimed directly at me—a slap on the ass, an unsolicited picture, but I never saw that happen. Instead, it was the subtle, meant-as-a-joke, stereotype-enforcing talk that I let slide.

A woman does need thick skin to work in fields where the gender demographic is similar to the ones I have worked in. It takes thick skin to take those comments and move on doing your job, showing yourself equal to and compatible with the guys. It takes a thicker skin to stand up and say something about those comments, showing them you won't take it. A thicker skin which I did not have at the time. It takes a backbone to say, "That is not okay to say." Even a simple, "What are you guys, twelve years old?" may have sufficed. Instead, I chose not to make a scene.

This is the reason that today, the sayings "being a pussy" and "having some balls" have opposite meanings.

All that being said, my overall experiences working dynamically alongside the guys rather than against them were positive and showed me there is still plenty of good in the world. Now get out there, kick some ass, and destroy those stereotypes!

BONUS ESSAY

A few years before publishing this book, I came across the service industry satire site, Sauce on the Side. I decided I'd give writing satire a shot, and I ended up being published a few times on their site! It's probably the closest thing to fiction I've written at this point. Here is one of my articles. Other headlines include, *"Female line cook tired of being asked if she's a server"* and *"Chef realizes steak gets more rest time than he does"*

You can find them all at ladylinecook.com

Chef pays his rent in compliments

ROCKLIN, CA — It has been reported that a line cook from pear-wasp's restaurant, Daniel Glenn, paid last month's rent with the compliments he has been receiving from guests.

"I heard that my co-workers in the front of the house were using their rewards for doing a good job to do things like pay rent, buy groceries, full up their tank, you know stuff like that," says Glenn, "so I thought, why shouldn't I?"

Witnesses say he handed over a large stack of "compliments," equivalent of about 500 US dollars as of this reporting. His landlord accepted the currency, and he was able to stay another month in his apartment.

"You'd think the people who actually made the food should get some kind of reward that has value in this world," says Glenn's co-worker, Steve Johnson, "Daniel is one of our best cooks here. Every night he works, all the servers are coming back to the kitchen giving him compliments on how great the food was."

"I don't even have to make the food and I get rewarded for how good it is," Says Sally Barton, a waitress at pear-wasp's, "It's amazing how the customer tells me how wonderful the risotto was and to give compliments to the chef, yet hands me the money that I get to keep!"

Glenn's landlord has declined to speak with the press regarding this story.

LET'S CONNECT!

Website:
www.ladylinecook.com

Instagram:
@ladylinecook

LADYLINECOOK

Facebook:
Hanalei Souza - Author

Twitter:
@theladylinecook